TRADITION
AND
INNOVATION

Selected Plenary and Panel Papers from the
Third Annual Conference of the Association for
Core Texts and Courses

Philadelphia, PA
10-13 April 1997

edited by

Scott Lee
Allen Speight

University Press of America,® Inc.
Lanham • New York • Oxford

Copyright © 1999
University Press of America,® Inc.
4720 Boston Way
Lanham, Maryland 20706

12 Hid's Copse Rd.
Cumnor Hill, Oxford OX2 9JJ

Library of Congress Cataloging-in-Publication Data

Association for Core Texts and Courses. Conference (3rd : 1997-
Philadelphia, Pa.)
Tradition and innovation : selected plenary and panel papers from
the Third Aannual Conference of the Association of Core Texts and
Courses, Philadelphia, PA. 10-13 April 1997 / edited by Scott Lee,
Allen Speight.
p.   cm.
1. Universities and colleges—United States—Curricula—
Congresses. 2. Curriculum planning—United States—Congresses.
I. Lee, J. Scott. II. Speight, Allen. III. Title.
LB2361.5.A86   1998   378.1'99'0973—dc21   98-49310 CIP

ISBN 0-7618-1308-X (cloth: alk. ppr.)
ISBN 0-7618-1309-8 (pbk: alk. ppr.)

⊖™ The paper used in this publication meets the minimum
requirements of American National Standard for Information
Sciences—Permanence of Paper for Printed Library Materials,
ANSI Z39.48—1984

Contents

γ

Preface

The present volume represents the first publication of *Selected Plenary and Panel Papers* from a conference of the Association for Core Texts and Courses (ACTC). The association, which first met in April 1995, takes as its mission to "bring together colleges and universities to promote the integrated and common study of world classics and other texts of major cultural significance."

The association was formed in large part because of the efforts of Stephen Zelnick and Scott Lee of Temple University. In the fall of 1994, Zelnick, who had recently become director of Temple's core-text Intellectual Heritage program, began to consider what sort of professional organization might be developed to fill the need for addressing the scholarly, pedagogical, and administrative issues involved in undergraduate core-text curricula. He and Lee organized the elements of what has become in the last three years an important resource for American and Canadian core programs. The association now includes some eighty institutions of higher learning, and has continued to provide an open and ongoing discussion on the need for core texts and core curricula.

The editors recognize the fervent debate in the academy on issues related to core texts and programs, and welcome a range of attempts to decide on what texts to use, what pedagogies are appropriate, and what curricula are successful. The wide academic debate about these issues may be represented by a question that Louise Cowan, from the University of Dallas, asked in her opening address to the 1997 Conference: what sort of story do our curricula now tell? As will be seen in this volume, the story is not univocal, although the many stories about core build a persuasive case for their use in higher education.

The educators who came to the conference represented the highly varied programs of core-text education on university, college, and community college campuses. Along with Cowan, other plenary speakers–Dennis O'Brien from the University of Dallas, Roger Shattuck from Boston University, and Gerald Graff from the University of Chicago–represent some of the breadth and diverse thinking that all ACTC members bring to general education and core texts.

The resulting dialogue among members aims to change North American education for the better. ACTC members come together to share their common concerns about core texts, courses, and curricula in order to stimulate the growth of core-text education. We have arranged the selected plenary and panel papers from the conference to reflect the conversations which took place among participants concerning the principles and methods of core-text education, as well as the interpretation and selection of the works used in such programs. Such conversations were the real work of the conference and, out of these, the growth of programs may well ensue. As the diverse programs of core curricula grow and mature, the Association for Core Texts and Courses looks forward to contributing to that growth and development.

* * *

Many ACTC colleagues offered suggestions and help in the preparation of this volume; to all, thanks. The editors wish to express particular gratitude to editorial assistants Leslie McGann, who helped with the initial phases of editing and paper selection, and William Lautzenheiser, whose computer skills and careful proofreading were invaluable for the final production of the volume.

SCOTT LEE
Temple University

ALLEN SPEIGHT
Boston University

Readers interested in other papers from this and earlier ACTC conferences may consult the ACTC Website at *http://acad.smumn.edu/ACTC/actc.html.*

Plenaries

The Need for Core

Roger Shattuck

Boston University

Permit me one preliminary observation.

Two days of attending panel discussions at this conference have convinced me that the ACTC stands for a much needed readjustment of our double commitment as professors to teaching and research. Most professional associations encourage specialized research far removed from the activity of teaching at the undergraduate level. Here, in contrast, every session I visited engaged in probing, high-level discussions of core authors, discussions addressed not to the conventions of originality that define pure research but to the application of advanced knowledge to the practicalities of curriculum, course design, and teaching in subjects vital to liberal education. Our undergraduate programs need this kind of scrutiny and sharing of pedagogical resources. This Association should do everything it can to assure that in assessments for salary, promotion, and tenure decisions, high quality in this kind of "applied" research receives recognition equal to that accorded to high quality in "pure" research. Such a readjustment will enhance the quality of undergraduate teaching and help restore an appropriate balance between teaching and research.

ᛒᛇᛜᛘᛝᛒᛝ

A pun, an amusing, useful, four-letter quibble, presides over our meeting today. I should like to savor that pun with you and put it to work in our discussion.

The best English dictionaries agree that the word *core* carries several meanings, including "an internal mould for a metal casting" and "a disease of the liver in sheep." We are concerned not with these specialized meanings but with two primary meanings, which form a nicely balanced opposition.

> **core**. A central portion that is cut out and rejected.
> **core**. The dry, horny capsule containing the seeds of apple, pear, quince, and other fruits.

I shall be returning to this quibble on core and to its usefulness.

In the United States we live in what is still, after two hundred years, a highly experimental system of government. Our attempt to establish democratic institutions, an equal system of justice, individual rights, and freedom of speech and religion remains a fragile undertaking that needs a great deal of intelligent care to continue. That understanding is threatened by those who see only its shortcomings, particularly among those who have grown up and been educated under this fledgling democracy. And it is threatened by those who preach that the cultures and interests of various segments of our population represent differences so significant that they can no longer be reconciled by the goals of democracy, justice, and freedom that have provided an ideal up to now. Do we want an integrated country seeking a national culture? Or do we want a resegregated country tending toward fragmentation into group interests?

It appears wise to me to found our education not on our most strident contemporary conflicts but on the trials and errors and slow accomplishments that have brought us to our imperfectly realized democratic institutions. Let us be clear that their history reaches back not merely two hundred years to our War of Independence, but four thousand years to the origins of Western civilization in the near East.

I wish to point out now that there are today at least four different ways of presenting and teaching core knowledge of the Western tradition. First, we have the Great Books format, in which a selection of works, often starting with Homer and the Old Testament, works its way gradually through Plato and Virgil, Machiavelli and Montaigne, Shakespeare and Milton, Rousseau and Goethe, and on toward the present. The list is not fixed or established (in my time, we read Cicero and Bunyan) yet it displays reasonable stability. Second, we have the appeal to big questions, to overarching themes: tradition and innovation; society and the individual; the emergence of scientific inquiry. Such questions reach very far.

The third way of teaching the Western tradition places at the center of the course not great works or themes but great historic and cultural junctures, periods of remarkable achievement in several domains. The choice is very large: the Eastern Mediterranean basin, cradle of civilizations; the Roman Empire; Christendom in the twelfth century; the Italian Renaissance; the court of the Sun King at Versailles; The Enlightenment in Western Europe; the Romantic revolt. Very difficult to plan and to teach coherently, such a course on cross-sections of history has the advantage of looking beyond high cultural production and of encouraging a comprehensive grasp of society at all levels.

The fourth and most recently devised way to teach the western tradition is best described by the copy that, since 1981, has accompanied Harvard's "Core Curriculum Program" (replacing General Education) and that provides the opening entry in the Harvard undergraduate catalogue, *Courses of Instruction*:

> The Core...does not define intellectual breadth as the mastery of a set of Great Books, or the digestion of a specific quantum of information, or the surveying of current knowledge in certain fields. Rather, the Core seeks to introduce students to the major *approaches to knowledge* in areas that the faculty considers indispensable to undergraduate education. It aims to show what kinds of knowledge and what forms of inquiry exist in these areas.

Derived from progressive education with its emphasis on "ways of thinking" and on skills rather than on knowledge, this "approaches to knowledge" program represents an unsound turn away from history, story, and verifiable fact toward abstraction and theory. It has not been successful at Harvard as a successor to General Education.

My own forty-year experience in designing and teaching core curricula and core courses leads me to believe that the traditional Great Books format serves both students and teachers best. No secondary version of an author's writing can substitute for the direct encounter with the words of Sophocles, of Augustine, of Voltaire. This close reading of original works can be combined with deep probes into the social functioning of key historical eras. "Approaches to Knowledge" or "ways of knowing" will come naturally to the fore in connection with figures like Aristotle and Galileo, Luther and Montaigne. The path itself, the curriculum, follows the core works that provide the content of the course.

In planning and administering a core program in the humanities, I believe that there is one sound pedagogic principle that will simplify many daunting problems. I mean the principle that has come to be called (after Horace and Pope) the hundred-year rule. The first, but not the only, test of a classic work is that it should have survived for a hundred years. Then we may begin to examine the qualities that give it that staying power. In application, this principle means that books written in the twentieth century have not yet passed the test and remain in limbo. Our four-semester core humanities course at Boston University closes with Nietzsche's *Beyond Good and Evil* and Dostoevsky's *Crime and Punishment*, in that reverse chronological order. The ideas and narratives of these two powerful authors comment on our current social, political, and moral dilemmas more cogently than most contemporary works. The faculty committee that designed the course finally agreed on three points. We would probably never reach consensus on which twentieth-century works to include. Even without entering the twentieth century, we didn't have enough room in the course for all the important authors before 1900. And most students would read Joyce and Virginia Woolf, Mann and Camus, Ellison and Faulkner, and possibly even Proust, in other courses. The further back you go in time, the simpler the choices seem to be. I admit to being still exercised over the omission in our core sequence of Frederick Douglass and of Charles Baudelaire. But that may change. And the authors we do read—including even Kant the killer whale—provide a feast I would not miss.

It is worth calling your attention at this point to one of the most widely accepted generalizations about college-level teaching in the United States. Colleges must serve the double function of transmitting the traditions, the disciplines, and the knowledge that make up our culture, and also of initiating an assessment and criticism of that culture. Logically and procedurally, the transmission function should precede the critical function; tradition comes before innovation and defines it. In two fields to which I am closely linked, history and literature, I detect a strong tendency today to reverse that order. For example, most freshman composition courses no longer emphasize students' writing: they undertake a systematic critique of contemporary culture and seek to change it.

The strong movement in history and English departments to criticize traditional knowledge even before it has been transmitted has encouraged a migration of teachers and courses toward cultural studies. The growth of this new field institutionalizes the ascendance of innovation and criticism over traditional knowledge and core works. Furthermore, cultural studies addresses itself almost exclusively to contemporary culture and contemporary writing about it. And the anti-literary egalitarian stance of cultural studies resists any evaluation that leads to the acknowledgment of a great book, a core work, a creation that lifts itself above the surrounding terrain. This double dismissal of the past and of literary quality goes a long way toward disqualifying cultural studies as a new discipline asking for recognition among existing disciplines in the humanities.

In many fields of study today, particularly in cultural studies, one comes across variations of the claim that *how* students read has far more importance than *what* they read. Such a claim attempts to remove in one pass any affirmation of a core within culture, any sustained attentiveness to that dry, horny capsule which contains the seeds and which we must never throw away. I would hesitate to claim priority either for what students read or for how they read. The two elements remain inseparable and essential. The important factor in reading at any level is that we try, on first reading, to set aside our prejudices and methods and approaches and to read without a program. The title piece in my book of essays is called "The Innocent Eye and the Armed Vision." We can never achieve the ideal of the innocent eye any more than the ideal of the disinterested attitude. But to begin reading with a good-faith attempt to achieve innocence and disinterest allows one to hear the author's voice sounding above our own cultural and personal limitations.

What students need to learn about reading is how to achieve and pursue this first encounter, not to make it conform to a critical approach, or to a political or sexist or minority point of view. All those categories as well as abstract theoretical terminology should be held off as long as possible and kept to a minimum in order to leave room for basics. And I must explain what I mean by basics.

A teacher must first ascertain whether students can fully construe a passage–understand the words and the sentence structure in their literal meaning. At any level of teaching, there will be misreadings. Then comes paraphrase. What is happening? To whom? With what effect? According to whom? Several paraphrases read aloud in the classroom reveal how widely students can differ about the literal meaning of a passage, before systematic interpretation even begins. To state that everything is always already interpreted reveals itself as a profoundly fatalistic and antipedagogical claim. The true teachers among us know that everything awaits interpretation anew every day.

The next step among my basics is reading aloud. To do so adequately requires understanding the rhythms, the pace, the shifting tone, and the subtleties of emphasis in a passage of prose or poetry. Oral interpretation demands great skill in the understanding and articulation of a work. All these forms of reading can take place in a classroom with students contributing to sustained examination of a chapter or passage. Through comparison with other works and other styles of writing, teachers and students can develop an appreciation of the potentialities and literary qualities of the written word.

One may, of course, direct such care in reading toward the most commercially driven and degraded writing a culture has produced, such as advertising and soap opera, and the process will lead to some results. But as long as cultures have recorded their history in spoken and written language, certain individuals have gained prominence as bards, as prophets, and as authors. There is an elementary act of faith that allows a young reader to respond to the voice of these superior authors. By convention, we refer to their works as literature. In our mission as teachers to transmit the core of our culture to the next generation, it is essential that the books we read with our students belong to this very diverse core of literary works. *What* we read is fully as important as *how* we read.

Can I say, then, what characterizes a great book? How does one recognize a literary classic by a superior author? I shall state a few rules of thumb; naturally they leave a large role for individual taste. A literary classic displays features that allow us to perceive in it elements both of simplicity, a rugged evidence about the forces in our lives, and of mystery, an acknowledgment of how complex the world truly is. Secondly, a literary classic makes its historical moment vivid and important and also reaches beyond the contingencies of any one era. It appeals to us simultaneously as a period piece and as a creation that remains forever young, forever timely. Lastly, a literary classic sets before us concrete, individual actions and characters, which at the same time take on the significance of the general, of the universal, in humanity.

As the fruit of long reading and reflection, these rules of thumb do not provide a rigid standard. They serve best to guide and encourage those who are still finding their way to the appreciation of literature. And let us here remember a fundamental principle that presides over our work in the humanities. The movement of thought in the humanities carries us ultimately not toward abstraction and general laws, as in the sciences, but toward individual works and events and persons in order to ascertain what is singular about them. On the principle that the basic unit of life and of value is the individual person, rooted in society and contingency and spirituality, we seek to recognize in literature the unique voice of the author at its most revealing pitch.

The first sentence of the organizing statement of this Association sets as its goal "to promote the integrated and common study of world classics and other texts of major cultural significance." My remarks have revealed that if I were drafting such a document, I should probably omit the last phrase, "and other texts of major cultural significance," as redundant and vague. And you will have registered my cordiality toward the analogy of the core for the kind of teaching most needed in our colleges today. Core works offer us both our traditions and the innovations that have gradually modified these traditions. The apple of literature in its fullest meaning, embracing the pun on "core," sets before us both the sweet pungency of its pulp and a more lasting reward in the dry, horny capsule that contains the seeds and that we shall not allow our students to throw away.

Response to Roger Shattuck

Gerald Graff

University of Chicago

Thank you for honoring me with your invitation to address this association and to debate Roger Shattuck, whose work I have long admired. While I was getting ready to come to this conference last week, I attended a family gathering and was asked by relatives where I would be going and what I'd be doing. Almost instantly I felt that constriction of the stomach muscles that sets in whenever I have to say something about what I do to nonacademics:

"I'm going to a conference in Philadelphia."

"Oh? A conference on what?"

"It's sponsored by a group called the Association for Core Texts and Courses."

"Sounds interesting. What do they do?"

"Well, you see there's been this big debate going on about the kinds of texts we teach in the academic humanities. You may actually have read about it?"

"Uh, no."

"Well, on the one hand, there has been a move of late to teach texts by African Americans, women, and other minorities. On the other hand, there's been a backlash coming from people who think we should get back to teaching the traditional canon of Western texts, you know, Shakespeare, and so forth. But the debate also involves questions about *how* we teach the texts, regardless which ones they are–that is, whether we raise political issues about gender and race and...."

Noting the blank expression of my relative, I had the familiar feeling once more of having failed to explain myself well and having disappointed my audience. Honestly curious, my relative asked me a simple question about what I do and I blew it.

In a way, I was relieved that my relatives knew nothing of the PC scandal and the canon debate. Evidently those (to my mind) wildly exaggerated accusations of political correctness against academics like me in op-ed pieces and best-sellers by writers like Allan Bloom and Dinesh D'Souza have not reached as wide an audience as I had feared. But it was small comfort to be reminded that it was only the obscurity of my concerns that protected my work from public exposure.

My relatives are not Philistines. They are relatively well-educated people, several with college degrees. They read serious literature, they go to plays, they like Shakespeare; they think of themselves as cultured people. But they feel complete outsiders to academic intellectual culture, whose discourse seems to them opaque and unfathomable.

In this respect, however, my relatives are in much the same position as most undergraduate college students (and certainly most high school students). And this is my excuse for dragging my unsuspecting relatives into my opening remarks today, because the problem posed by the gulf between me and them seems to me more fundamental and educationally more important than the issues that have monopolized our attention in the great debate over "core texts" and courses. In that debate, we have become so caught up in the combat between traditional books and nontraditional books that we have lost sight of the fact that, for most American students and most Americans generally, the problem has always been the culture of books and book-discussion *as such*, regardless which faction gets to draw up the reading list. If, like my relatives and most students, you are intimidated and confused by the culture of book-discussion, you are likely to be alienated from the academic study of books regardless whether the books are traditional or multicultural.

Another way to make my point is to refer you to what I think of as the "Cliffs Notes" problem. In the last few years some of the most widely-assigned texts by minority writers, including such works as Alice Walker's *The Color Purple*, Amy Tan's *The Joy Luck Club*, and Maya Angelou's *I Know Why the Caged Bird Sings* have been appearing in Cliffs Notes. Such a development, it seems to me, raises an awkward question for those in favor of canon-revision: will it profit you to get Alice Walker and Maya Angelou into course reading lists if students are just as dependent on Cliffs Notes for dealing with these new texts as they have always been for dealing with Shakespeare and Milton?

The point, however, cuts two ways: what will it profit traditionalists to keep the canon safe for Shakespeare and Milton, that is, to keep Walker and Angelou out, if their students still need the Cliffs Notes in order to make a literate statement about these classics? Unless such questions are raised, there is a serious danger that the outcome of the canon debate will be simply to reshuffle the contents of the curriculum while the gulf between student culture and intellectual culture stays as wide as ever, and the fundamental educational problem is not affected. The more things change in terms of texts, the more they will have stayed the same in terms of how the texts are understood.

Of course, not all students are estranged from academic intellectual culture. In most college classes, a group emerges that I have come to think of as the "Fifteen Percent Club": students who, through family background, church, or whatever source, have already been more-or-less socialized into the intellectual club before they arrive on campus. These students are already proto-intellectuals, having a feeling for how to talk about books, culture, and ideas. The other eighty-five percent, however, harbors much the same feeling of exclusion as my relatives do: they may enjoy reading the assigned books, but they are not able to follow or to produce the kind of book-talk in which the professors and the Fifteen Percent Club engage.

All of this suggests why it is important to shift the emphasis in our curricular debates from the question of which texts we teach, or even according to which theories we teach them, to the way academic intellectual culture *talks about* texts and other matters. The most fundamental gap, finally, is not the one between clashing texts and theories–for to enter that clash of texts and theories you already have to be a member of the intellectual club–but between those who talk the talk of academic intellectual culture and those who do not.

Academic intellectual talk is distinguished by its high degree of self-consciousness, its analytical distance, and the premium it places on the formulation of allegorical meanings and implications, whether the abject of study is a Shakespeare sonnet, a TV commercial, a psychiatric case study, or an economic trend. Academic intellectual talk is heavily "meta"–it is always reflecting metadiscursively back on itself and its own concepts, generating talk about talk about talk to an extent that seems off-putting or puzzling to outsiders. It is this obsessive concern to construct meta-allegories that has always dismayed students in literature courses, spurring the familiar complaints about literature teachers' insistence that "hidden meaning" or "symbolism" be found in every text, or about those teachers' apparent habit of "reading too much into" everything. What students and other nonacademics find unclear is why it is so necessary for academics to "intellectualize" about books, instead of simply reading them for fun.

From the outside, academic analytic reading processes look like kind of misplaced dentistry, in which a helpless text is subjected to a complex methodological machine for the extraction of little of apparent value. The malaise provoked by the process is similar whether the analytic methodology in question is Old-fashioned and traditional or new-fangled and "transgressive." In other words, it is the academic modes of reading and talking about reading–indeed, the very idea that there are different "modes of reading" that can be objects of debate in their own right–that stick in the craw of the nonacademic, whether the mode be the more traditional kind of reading Roger Shattuck might feel comfortable with, or a Marxist, feminist, or deconstructionist reading. For an academic insider, the difference between these modes of reading is vast, but they look virtually indistinguishable to the outsider, for whom academic reading as such seems strange. In the dark, all methodologies are gray.

Though we sometimes push it to Byzantine lengths, it seems to me that our close, analytical reading of texts and our metareflection about it are things we academics do well, and are part of the contribution we make to the larger culture. But we have done a poor job of transmitting this skill of reading and reflecting and its larger rationale to those outside the already-initiated minority of our students. Thus again it would be healthy to reorient the Great Book debate away from what books we read and how we read them to how we talk about what we read. After all, it is only through a student's oral or written account that we have any way of assessing what his or her reading experience has been. Operationally, it is what students *say* about their reading that matters, and if students don't command the vocabulary for making statements about books, their reading will be impoverished.

My assumption here is that one of the primary goals of teaching must be to help or induce students to become intellectuals, which is to say, to socialize them into the culture of book-talk, of historical reflection, of metadiscursive argument. Teachers' success in accomplishing this goal is quite independent of whether students become conservative intellectuals, traditional intellectuals, leftist intellectuals, or middle-of-the-road intellectuals. It's not that I don't care what my students believe, but my job as an educator is to convert students to the intellectual life, not to try to determine the intellectual faction they ally with. This philosophy should especially makes sense if you agree that at present only a small minority of American students become intellectual insiders and the rest feel shut out, or prefer to be shut out.

Steve Zelnick, I understand, spoke earlier to this group about what rhetoric and composition specialist Peter Elbow calls "the Belief Game," giving provisional credence to beliefs that you don't actually hold or even find repugnant in order to learn what it feels like to entertain perspectives different from your own. The Belief Game seems to me a very useful notion, but in order to play it well students need to control the vocabularies of argument in which intellectual beliefs are formulated and exchanged. Helping students to control these intellectual vocabularies should therefore take priority for teachers over worrying about whether those student beliefs end up being closer to the beliefs of Roger Shattuck or of me. Again, the texts and cultural philosophies are less important than whether students acquire the language for discussing texts and philosophies.

These are principles that many on the cultural Left and the Right should be able to agree on. Though consensus on educational issues is obviously important, we have been looking for consensus in the wrong place–in texts and philosophies rather than in the intellectual discourse through which texts and philosophies must be filtered. Few of the combatants on any side in today's culture war would dispute the proposition that it is a good thing to socialize students more effectively into the intellectual conversation
of our culture. This latent agreement on the importance of intellectual discourse, which includes not just academics, but journalists, media people, politicians, and other literate people, is something we could build on if we could overcome our fixation on texts.

Roger Shattuck described a program at Boston University that decided it had to eliminate the twentieth century from its curriculum because it could not get agreement on which twentieth-century texts it should teach. This seems a symptom of the unnecessary paralysis that results from looking for consensus in the wrong place. What would it profit the BU faculty if it got full consensus on all the texts to be taught if only a minority of its students were able to write a coherent interpretation of those texts without reliance on Cliffs Notes? On the other hand, if BU students acquire the ability to interpret texts cogently and articulately, they can then be trusted to make intelligent responses to a variety of texts. Once you see that it is not the texts that matter so much as what the students are able to do with the texts, the pressure on the faculty to agree on every text is relieved.

Another reason why it is self-defeating to make curricular decisions hinge on getting consensus on what texts to teach lies in the changed conditions of publishing over the last generation. The expansion of the canon that makes it so difficult to agree on texts came about not primarily because of insurgent academic canon-busters, but because of a publishing explosion since the paperback revolution of the late 1950s. If we must blame someone for the canon controversy, we should let up on the academics and start blaming the publishers: once cheap editions became widely available, it was natural and predictable that they would be assigned in courses, thereby greatly expanding the academic canon.

A far greater quantity of literate culture presents itself today for teaching than was available in 1950, yet the amount of time in which to teach it has not has not expanded at all. Under these expanded conditions, to go on thinking that we have to get full agreement on the texts we assign in order to teach effectively, is all the more a prescription for paralysis.

Another academic habit of thought that does not help matters is one that would discourage students from reading secondary works, criticism, and theory on the ground that too much exposure to such secondary material will come between the students and the great texts. A variant of this view—one that reflects a distorted recognition of the Cliffs Notes problem—is the belief that the only use most students can make of criticism is to plagiarize from it. Another variant springs from the mistaken assumption that if book is truly great, it will somehow tell the student what he or she is supposed to say about it without the need for any mediating language of critical response. What this assumption ignores is that it is mastery of critical discourse, including a sense of what other literate people have been saying about the book in question, that gives readers a sense of what they can say about the books. Whatever its motivations, discouraging students from reading criticism is a self- destructive tactic, since its effect is to withhold from students the very discourse that they are expected to produce and are penalized for not producing. Again, since the only way students can demonstrate the quality of their reading experience is through what they say about it, withholding the discourse of criticism from them virtually assures that their accounts will be impoverished.

Finally, another way academic institutions make it hard for students to join our intellectual community is in the mixed messages that result from the disconnected nature of the curriculum. Students typically experience a form of radical cognitive dissonance as they move from course to course and are exposed to wild contradictions and discrepancies of perspective that rarely intersect in any clarifying dialogue. It is rather as if you were to try to learn Chinese while also trying to learn several different Chinese dialects that cannot communicate with each other. It is hardly surprising in the circumstances that many students cope by giving each teacher the viewpoint he or she seems to "want" even when these viewpoints are flatly contradictory. Students in this way become adept at being traditionalists in their ten o'clock class, radicals in their eleven o'clock, and middle-of-the-roaders after lunch.

If relativism is a problem in education today, as so many believe it is, I suspect its deepest cause lies not in the relativistic philosophies expounded by teachers (though some of these do exist), but in a conventional curriculum that presents students with an increasingly diverse and dissonant variety of perspectives with little chance to see the differences worked through in a direct conversation. The only way to counteract curricular cognitive dissonance (short of purging the curriculum of its variety of perspectives) is to bring the clashing perspectives together for students under conditions that enable them to enter the debate–something that again comes back to the need to provide students with the discourse of argumentation and analysis that enables one to make such comparisons.

Here I believe I'm in disagreement with Roger and his defense (admittedly qualified) of the idea of the "innocent eye." I believe that our experience of anything is always mediated by an interpretation, all the more when we give an account of our experience to others. So no matter how faithfully a teacher may stick to "the text itself" what the student is exposed to is inevitably some person's interpretation and sooner or later a conflict or interplay of interpretations. Keeping students screened from this conflict and interplay of interpretations only makes it difficult for them to enter interpretive discussions and, by extension, to read well.

To put my argument most succinctly, it will not matter much who wins the canon debate if we in academic institutions do not create a culture of argument at the center of the curriculum that students can join and want to join. I believe that one means to this end would be to create student versions of the kind of academic conference we are taking part in now, and I am pleased that students are participating in this conference. At the University of Chicago, I have been involved in organizing such student conferences at various levels, from graduate students to high school students, including conferences in which different levels of students interact. Another path to the same end is the "learning community" strategy of clustering of courses, a version of which is being developed locally at Temple University under the leadership of Classics Professor Dan Tompkins (who chaired a session on learning communities just this morning). In my experience, nothing more effectively socializes students into the culture of argument than doing the sort of thing we are doing right here as we publicly present our arguments, listen to the arguments of others, and engage one another's differences. Furthermore, asking students to join such arguments in turn puts the responsibility on us teachers to train students and ourselves to become better arguers.

I believe this goal of creating a more coherent culture of argument in the curriculum is one on which traditionalists, radicals, and middle-of-the-roaders in the culture war can agree. We are not likely to agree very soon about which books should be taught or how they should be taught. What we can realistically hope to agree on is the need to bring students more fully than they have been into our intellectual discussion about books. And in my view, to accomplish that end would be an educational success of great significance.

Set It Down with Gold on Lasting Pillars:

The Fallacy of Misplaced Concreteness in the Undergraduate Curriculum

Louise Cowan

University of Dallas

Let me begin by saying that my assumption is that I am preaching to the choir; that is, most of you here are likely to be in favor of a core curriculum of some sort, a conviction which no doubt separates you partially, at least, from most of your colleagues in America. An article in *USA Today* about a year ago reports that the National Association of Scholars found that, in 1993, among fifty top U.S. colleges only fourteen percent had some type of literature requirement; twelve percent required history; the same percentage, math.[1] As we all know, the curricular situation is dire indeed, and, as we also suspect, it will be by those of us who believe in some variety of general requirements for all undergraduates that the collapse of higher education in this country will be averted.

Yet, if the university's curriculum today is in shambles, it is at least partly so because those who have defended a traditional curriculum have held too narrow a position–and in so doing have confused an unchanging and quite tangible inherited structure with the intangibles that must be taught. I would, therefore, focus my remarks on what is wrong with the academic tendency to preserve the curricular *status quo*, suggesting that when we set ourselves rigidly against change we tend to

erect an idol; and idols are all too easily overturned. Those of us who
have some sense of the importance of a tradition need to recognize its
essential fluidity, its ability to accommodate itself to diversity. Addressing this issue I have entitled my remarks (borrowing from Shakespeare's *Tempest*): "Set It Down with Gold on Lasting Pillars: The
Fallacy of Misplaced Concreteness in the Undergraduate Curriculum."

After the trials and struggles on Prospero's and Caliban's island, the
good old lord Gonzalo sums up the mind of the entire company when
he says:

> O, rejoice
> Beyond a common joy, and set it down
> With gold on lasting pillars: In one voyage
> Did Claribel her husband find at Tunis
> And Ferdinand, her brother, found a wife
> Where he himself was lost, Prospero his dukedom
> In a poor isle and all of us ourselves
> When no man was his own.

How we defenders of what we consider the traditional curriculum tend
to wish that it could be preserved forever!–as do the authors of such
books as *The Closing of the American Mind, Illiberal Education, Killing the Spirit, Impostors in the Temple, Tenured Radicals*, and (it
seems) countless other volumes. How we wish we could set down the
curriculum the way it used to be "with gold on lasting pillars." But the
mistake Gonzalo makes is the same mistake he made earlier on the island, when he took its primordial reality to be a mere political opportunity to build a Utopia on rational and abstract principles, rather than
seeing in it a radical potential for change:

> I' the commonwealth I would by contraries
> Execute all things.
> . . . .
> All things in common nature should produce
> Without sweat or endeavor: treason, felony,
> Sword, pike, knife, gun, or need of any engine,
> Would I not have; but nature should bring forth,
> Of its own kind, all foyson, all abundance,
> To feed my innocent people.

His benevolent but simplistic mind literalizes the strange conditions of
the island, failing to recognize in this primal place a region of creativity–where imagination encounters powers beyond human reason and
clears the way for metamorphosis. As Ariel sings:

> Full fathom five thy father lies;
>   Of his bones are coral made;
> Those are pearls that were his eyes;

Nothing of him that doth fade
But doth suffer a sea-change
Into something rich and strange.

All the castaways subjected to the magic of the island are to be re-made, to suffer a sea change. They are not to be *taught* so much as *transformed*. The true issue of the experience is summed up not in Prospero's books, but in the wonder that is Miranda. Her coming marriage to Ferdinand, the Prince of Naples, offers good reason to hope for the continuance of the human race. Prospero, the teacher, in preparing his daughter for life, has subjected her to the fearful fens and bogs of the island, the sensuality of Caliban, his own account of a troubled past in the old world, and a test of her ability to recognize love as commitment. Finally, Prospero himself, as the teacher who continues to learn, must come to forgive his enemies, divest himself of special powers, accept Caliban as part of himself, and return to active life a changed person. For, as he has found, wisdom is not to be equated with his arcane learning from the Old World or with texts in themselves. The drowning of his books is a necessary admission of his own status as a continual learner, not mere dispenser of learning.

Miranda is both the inspirational Beatrice figure pursued in education and the end-product, the daughter who embodies the hope for human culture–like Shakespeare's Portia and Imogen, James's Isabel Archer, Faulkner's Linda Snopes in *The Town* and *The Mansion*, Toni Morrison's Denver in *Beloved*, and Isabel Allende's Alba in *The House of Spirits*. Alba, in twentieth-century Chile, the granddaughter of a politically conservative *patron* and daughter of a revolutionist, survives imprisonment, rape, and torture, and at the end of the novel bears within her a child of unknown parentage. She has come home to her dying grandfather, the figure of the tyrannical old order, and in caring for him, has come across her grandmother's letters. Like Miranda, Alba has been educated by the past, not to duplicate it but to redeem it:

> It would be very difficult for me to avenge all those who should be avenged [she writes], because my revenge would be just another part of the same inexorable rite. I have to break that terrible chain. I want to think that my task is life and that my mission is not to prolong hatred but simply to fill these pages while I wait for Miguel, while I bury my grandfather, whose body lies beside me in this room, while I wait for better times to come, while I carry this child in my womb, the daughter of so many rapes or perhaps of Miguel, but above all, my own daughter.

She struggles, here, to make sense of her own destiny, using the materials given to her–her grandmother's letters, her grandfather's political despotism, her father's battles for the poor and dispossessed–along with commands from her dead grandmother in an apparition during her most desperate moments in prison. Such texts, as we might call these bodies of knowledge gain from sources other than one's own direct experience, provide the discrepant matter to be studied, conveying to the young the stories of their many-times painful heritage. History is essentially tragic. But it can be redeemed by imagination. Hence, the educational aim is not so much transmission of content as the awakening of imagination and insight. The curriculum becomes the means for that awakening and, as such, should aim at making itself finally invisible.

Hence, just as it is insufficient to make education a matter of equipping students with skills or information, so it is insufficient to endow them with the ability to converse about a privileged content–even Plato or Aristotle, Homer or Dante. Such cultural literacy may be an incidentally desirable trait, but it is not the principal reason for education. Rather, we should wish our students to be transformed by having studied seriously a wide variety of texts so that they embody and extend the ongoing of wisdom in the world. The curriculum itself is not sacrosanct, not an end in itself; instead, it is a means of evoking a necessary inner knowledge for the survival of the human species.

But in the culture wars of the last few years, the very concept of curriculum is in jeopardy. In our time curricular issues tend to be primarily those that raise consciousness: questions of power, gender, and ethnicity. Having lost the last vestiges of an already attenuated course of studies, we now stand before an empty syllabus with only personal whim or political commitment to guide us. Traditionalists continue making such well-meaning mistakes as designing compendia courses that by sampling and generalization attempt to give students an overview. Or they try the distribution method: so many hours in this area, so many in that. In contrast, innovators introduce materials addressing social issues they desire to change. The curriculum thus comes to be considered primarily in a political light, to be approached as an instrument of either conservation or reform. It thus becomes to some a canon, a model, a guide to culture; to others a dossier detailing abuses, an arena for contention, a political agenda.

Now I would emphasize that neither the traditionists nor the progressivists in this battle are blameless. Those who would set down with gold on lasting pillars the curriculum as they think it has been in better days would make of it a walled fortress blocking our way rather than a path opening into the future; on the other hand, those who would have it fluctuate with every passing gale of political unrest would subject us in a leaky boat to the chaotic patterns of the uncharted sea. What are we Prosperos in the academy to do confronted with such irreconcilable conflict? How are our Mirandas and our Albas to be educated?

As Lawrence Lavine points out in his *Opening of the American Mind*, the curriculum has never been a stable thing. It has always been subject to the kind of reformulation that keeps a tradition alive. Those who would decry any changes in it run the risk of an idolatry that obstructs the lifeblood of education, rendering it–the whole process–sclerotic. But those who would govern the course of studies by whim or personal preference, adding courses in curiosity or in rage as they seem to be momentarily interesting or disturbing, loose the blood-dimmed tide, so that institutions of higher learning drained of significance may finally die of irrelevance. The issue is crucial. How do we keep what is good of the past and yet allow the entrances of the new? How do we do justice to the dynamic process of learning?

Let me posit a few of my own convictions for curricular reform (gained from five decades of working with curricula) which we may consider during the conference and, perhaps, continue to clarify (or dismiss) afterward:

First: *The distinction between liberal studies and illiberal education needs to be maintained but rethought.* Education sought for its own sake needs still to be defended against careerism. Colleges and universities do not exist primarily to develop a work force for society. Apprenticeships in business and industry must serve that need. Yet, the liberal arts approach as it has been defined in the past–as the education of a gentleman–is no longer completely adequate. As Bruce Kimball points out in his *Orators and Philosophers*, the term has never meant solely one thing in its long tradition. But however we choose to interpret the word *liberal*, the concept of knowledge as primarily an *intellectual* good is hardly adequate for our drastic situation today. The good of the mind is, no doubt, the immediate aim of learning, but the ultimate aim needs to be *paideia*, the development of the soul. Purposes are at work in a good curriculum that entail far more than intellectual development.

Second: *A common core ought to be required for all students at each college or university.* Liberal education is not to be found in books; it is to be found in community in a classroom, an artificial environment like Prospero's island. George H. Douglas in *Education without Impact* quotes the philosopher Santayana as replying to the question of what books students should read with the answer, "It doesn't really matter very much what they read–except that they should all read the same things." Such a statement is not, of course, meant to be taken seriously. But there is something to his remark.

Each text offers opportunities for extrapolation into a large "myth" in which students dwell during their four years of undergraduate days. Such a myth–unlike philosophic or political principles–encourages diversity within coherence. Myths are largely unexpressed and hence flexible. But they are vitally needed in the process of education, so that a common discourse may prevail, whatever the differences or opinions may be, whatever the outside world may be like. Lacking this mutual experience, graduates remain undeveloped; their fund of ideas shallow and curtailed. As the Russian critic Bakhtin has written, ideas exist only in dialogue, in the exchange between persons. Without this sense of a commonly shared universe of discourse, ideas remain unexplored, unprobed, hardening finally into prejudices, held unthinkingly, or into their opposite, cynicism and apathy. The curriculum ought to require certain whole texts that every student reads and discusses, not simply selections from areas of study.

Third: *Most of the texts chosen should be, by common acceptance, classics.* Nothing can serve the two purposes of education–the construction of a cosmos and the apprehension of one's true self–quite like the classic texts of Western civilization–which are classic precisely because they have had this kind of awakening effect on readers throughout the ages; and because America has been shaped by the ancient and European world, most classics should probably come from that tradition. We need to acknowledge again the primacy of the Greeks–however not simply to learn Greek literature or Greek philosophy, but to learn about ourselves. As Werner Jaeger writes in his classic *Paideia,*

> We return to Greece because it fulfills some need in our own life....The theoria of Greek philosophy...embodied not only rational thought...but also...vision, which apprehended every object as a whole, which sees the idea in everything–namely visible pattern.

The pattern was a living ideal, but as Jaeger points out "it would be a very grave mistake to imagine that the ideal was ever fixed and final."

Classics from other cultures need to be added, of course–the choice not based on a sociological standard, but on the standard of quality and even more important on the completion of the human image. As works become important to us in our culture, we should add them judiciously to the curriculum. The great texts are by their very nature intertextual; the large genres mentioned by Aristotle in the *Poetics,* tragedy, epic, comedy, and lyric, naturally gather their kindred to themselves over the years. Introduce Derek Walcott's *Omeros* to a course on epic and *The Iliad, The Odyssey, The Aeneid,* and *The Divine Comedy* all sit up and take notice of what the Caribbean experience adds to their meaning. Include Wole Soyinka in a course on tragedy and see the total import of the course alter. End a course in the novel with Toni Morrison's *Beloved*–and watch the way in which themes hitherto undiscovered in the other works come to life in high relief. Add Ralph Ellison's "Fly Away Home," Gabriel Garcia-Marquez's "A Very Old Man With Enormous

Wings," or Toni Morrison's *Song of Solomon* to a course in epic and see the resonances that play back and forth between the texts.

Fourth: *The curriculum is actually, in Aristotle's terms, the mythos, the plot that best imitates the action.* The plot of a work of art (of a tragedy, as he is describing it, but he means it to apply to all literary fictions) is the most important element. But the plot is not the action. The plot *imitates* the action: it is a metaphor of the action, a model, an analogy. The action that the story embodies. The action that the story embodies is an invisible movement of spirit, as Francis Fergusson has put it. There could be many possible plots for the same action that the artist seeks to depict (as we find from reading the journals of a writer such as Dostoevsky). If we think of the curriculum as the plot, then we become more aware of the overall arrangement that it must have: it cannot be a mere aggregate, a collection of examples, a sampling from the many cultures of the world, no matter how worthy the parts collected.

What sort of story does the curriculum tell? For the Greeks, it told the story of eros searching for the beautiful; for the Romans, its story was Aeneas' kind of *amor*, love of duty, of *patria*; for the Medieval citizen, the story was one of the metaphysical nature of love; since the Renaissance, out story has been the Faustian desire for infinite knowledge. Our problem with the curriculum at this moment is that we have lost our story. We don't know what our myth is. We don't know what we love, as Augustine would put it. It is this fundamental uncertainty about the mission of our society that more than anything else has threatened our educational systems and decimated our curricula.

Despite our loss of a generally agreed upon overview, the curriculum within our institutions of learning must still tell stories; they have to be in motion, following the ancient laws of complication and resolution. It is not enough to expose various subjects and points of view; it is not enough to teach students "to think," to examine data critically; it is not enough to impart a sophisticated skepticism that detaches the student from the experiences from which he learns. The curriculum must tell a story that both unfolds itself in the learner's psyche and develops a cosmos in which his or her mind can find room for its many turnings.

Fifth: *The curriculum has to regain its power to invoke belief.* As teachers, we have to recapture faith in what we teach–and show it. We have to believe in something beyond the text that the text can manage to convey.

Some time back the theologian Paul Tillich spoke of three types of education: technical, humanist, and inducting. The first, which teaches skills and practices, is always with us; the second, humanist, begun in the Renaissance, has now declined to a hollow shell of itself. The kind of education desperately needed in our time, he maintains, is inducting:

the sort that leads a student into a coherent world view; the kind that makes a student say, as the torso of Apollo said to Rilke, "You must change your life."

Robert E. Proctor, in his book *Education's Great Amnesia* would agree with Tillich:

> The tradition of classical education, which began in the Renaissance and flourished in Europe and America until the end of the last century, is gone now. How should we react to the death of this tradition? We can either mourn it and try to hold on to it, or we can see its passing as a liberation and as an opportunity for us to appropriate the past in new ways. (xviii)

Sixth: *We need to investigate more deeply, then, the disciplinary approach–a reenactment of the medieval liberal arts.* Such a method explores the laws of thought in and of themselves, as they relate to the different disciplines, not simply in their relation to a cultural tradition. We need to be able to make the distinction, as Donald Cowan points out in *Unbinding Prometheus*, between education and learning. Education is enculturation, concerned to endow students with their cultural legacy; learning is timeless, concerned with the laws of being. All students are entitled to an experience of learning. As Jacques Maritain has written, the true task of education is "the awakening of the learner's intuitive power."

The disciplinary approach remains the most effective way to develop the full powers of insight. A discipline is a mode of thinking, a path to knowledge guided by its own laws. Jerome Bruner has written in *The Relevance of Education*:

> The disciplines of learning represent not only codified knowledge, but ways of thought, habits of mind, implicit assumptions, short cuts, and styles of humor that never achieve explicit statement....These ways of thought keep knowledge lively, keep the knower sensitive to opportunity and anomaly. (16-17)

Seventh: *Along with a heightened sense of the disciplines as modes of thought, not as bodies of content, education must regain a sense of having an interdisciplinary context.* But the disciplines interact, they do not merge. By means of different "voices," students may gain a polymorphic instead of a monological imagination. The best interdisciplinary connections are to be found within the student body itself–and even more, within the student's own mind.

Eighth: *We need to consider again the power of poetry as an organizing principle of the curriculum.* The fundamental flaw in most educational systems is the literalization of curriculum, hence literalization of the mind. The conviction that students are prepared for living in the contemporary world by being taught contemporaneity underestimates the ability of the mind to work by analogy–to apply what it has learned theoretically to the practical world around it.

Poetry aids in the making of an analogy, the formation of a cosmos; it provides a detached ability to see the whole; a passionate involvement with the self. Werner Jaeger's perception of the reciprocity between literature and ancient education and culture are applicable to our own day: "The ancients were persuaded that education and culture are not a formal art or an abstract theory, distinct from the objective historical structure of a nation's spiritual life. They held them to be embodied in literature, which is the real expression of all higher culture."

Ninth: *We need to reassess the true aims of education; to produce the good person; the fully human man or woman, of whatever race, of whatever gifts.* American colleges and universities have played an increasingly important role in the national destiny; and at the end of the twentieth century it is of crucial importance for those who form curricula to accept the responsibility of ascertaining standards. They need to make clear to themselves and to the world that the educational task of the University is not so much the teaching of a certain body of material as the quest for the full human image. And in a nation dedicated to pluralism, with a constituency increasingly diverse, that image is not to be discerned by a sampling.

Tenth: *Finally, we need to remember what Mortimer Adler has ingrained in all of us: "The best education is the best for all."* Honors courses are a step in the right direction, but they are not the answer to our problem. American education is in its very soul democratic. It cannot continue to use an elitist Renaissance model; it must return to its sources in Greece and Rome, as well as look outward to those countries never industrialized and yet moving now into the global culture–countries where an oral tradition and ancient myths still abound.

We educators might describe ourselves as being in the same position as Prospero: we've given too much time to our private specializations, and find ourselves adrift in a leaky boat, with our books, our robes, our young. The sea bears no trace of human history; everything has been obliterated in it; there are only the intricate fractals and strange nuances of chaos. If we come at last to an island, finding ourselves thus in a kind of classroom, what shall we teach? The knowledge of that old world we left behind, the arcane knowledge preserved in our books, the primal knowledge to be found on the island–from both Caliban and Ariel; or that which is fundamental to us all: the unchanging laws of human nature–the good grasped by the imagination, analyzed by the intellect, shared in community, and embodied, finally, in the living human ideal?

At the end of *The House of Spirits*, Alba is putting together her story from her grandfather's notebooks, who wrote, as she said, because memory is fragile and the space of a single life is brief, passing so quickly that we never get a chance to see the relationship between events; we cannot gauge the consequences of our acts, and we believe in the fiction of past, present, and future, but it may also be true that everything happens simultaneously.

In the imagination that must shape our lives, all does. Thus, though we need texts–testimonials from others–the end product is not the grandmother's letters–the texts–but the living person reading them who is attempting to make a life. The trouble with setting it down with gold on lasting pillars is the fallacy of misplaced concreteness: we make a monument an end of something that should be a means, something that should be shifting, adjusting itself in its turns toward the new life to which it is directed.

Note

1. Dennis Kelly, "Colleges Chip Away at Core Courses," *USA Today*, 19 March 1996.

The Core Curriculum:

It Is Music to My Ears

Dennis O'Brien

Middlebury College

I begin these remarks with my favorite collegiate lawsuit, *Trustees of Columbia University* v. *Jacobsen*, 53. N.J. Super (Superior Court of New Jersey, 1959). It seems that one Jacobsen failed to pay his tuition to Columbia University. The University sued for payment, but Jacobsen filed a counterclaim in fifty counts alleging fraud. Columbia, so claimed Jacobsen,

> had represented that it would teach...wisdom, truth, character, enlightenment, understanding, justice, liberty, honesty, courage, beauty and similar virtues and qualities; that it would develop the whole man, maturity, well roundedness, objective thinking and the like; and that because it had failed to do so it was guilty of misrepresentation.

Officials of Columbia testified at the trial that by no means did the University claim to provide such lofty goals for its students. Jacobsen, acting as his own attorney, countered by citing the Columbia College Catalogue: "Columbia College provides a liberal arts education... which has extremely positive value of its own...It develops the whole man...." Jacobsen quoted from the president's convocation address: "There can never have been a time in the history of the world when men have greater need for wisdom...To this task, Columbia like other great centers of learning...unhesitatingly dedicates itself." Jacobsen even noted the inscription on the college chapel: "Wisdom dwelleth in the heart of him that has understanding." Why, he asked, if Columbia University doesn't teach wisdom does it go about advertising it on its buildings? I am sorry to say that Jacobsen lost. The appellate judge summed up: "wisdom is not a subject which can be taught and no rational person would accept such a claim made by any man or institution."

Jacobsen was not a lone eccentric. I graduated from an institution whose motto is "For God, for Country, and for Yale." At the same time that Jacobsen was reading inscriptions at Morningside Heights, William F. Buckley took Yale's motto literally and, in a notorious book, *God and Man at Yale,* denounced the institution for betraying God, country, and Yale's educational mission. The authorities at Yale were as dismissive of Buckley as the judges of the New Jersey Appellate division were of Jacobsen.

Despite judicial ruling, it seems to me that there is a nagging worry about the Jacobsen case. What are we to make out of all those grand claims for God and country and light and wisdom? Wouldn't it be better just to quietly retire these high flown mottoes, get the chisel out and erase aspiration from the architecture lest we mislead our clientele?

Those grand epigrams were, of course, the product of a different age in American higher education, the age of the denominational Christian college. The basic purpose of the old-style institutions was moral and religious–thus all those elevated mottoes. Moral discipline, religious revival, and the college as ethical tutor *in loco parentis* all fit the philosophy of the denominational college. Knowing the Gospel message, all one needed was enforcement to sustain its message. Mark Hopkins, the legendary president of Williams College, opined that there was only one book needed in the library: the Bible.

The curriculum of the nineteenth-century college conformed to its overall correctional aim. Not only were moral habits sternly pressed in everyday life, the mode of instruction was recitation of classic texts. These cullings from ancient authors served two purposes: they were set as exemplars of proper literary style *and* depictions of good republican habits. One learned not only Cicero's periodic style, but admired his opposition to anti-republican conspiracy.

I remind you of this ancient history of American higher education because I want to examine–and in part rehabilitate–the pedagogy of the past. At first glance–and probably even with a steady gaze–one would not hold much of a brief for collegiate old style. This wasn't education, it was indoctrination. Yes, I think that is basically correct, and I doubt that anyone wants to go back to a curriculum composed exclusively of late Latin authors and Paley's *Natural Theology: or Evidences of the Existence and Attributes of the Deity.* But before we chuck the classical college once and for all, we should understand its underlying rationale. That rationale can be best revealed and appreciated by considering the research university revolution which replaced the denominational college of yore. The modern research university–the model which defines virtually all of American higher education from the great universities to the smallest colleges–can be differentiated from its predecessor by at least three contrasts: academic discipline versus religious denomination, science versus Faith, discovery versus recovery.

There are many facets to the modern research revolution, but the controversy over Darwin at the end of the last century encapsulates the whole story. The academic discipline of biology quite displaced the Biblical story of Adam and Eve. Part and parcel of disciplinary ascendancy was the triumph of what Max Weber aptly called the "ascetic" method of the modern academy. Leopold von Ranke, the founder of modern "scientific" history, wished to distinguish his work from the propagandistic chronicles which had preceded him. Historical writing for Ranke was to describe "*Wie es eigentlich gewesen war*," how things really were. The personal faiths, political commitments, and social placement of the investigator were to be radically transcended in search of the truth as it is. Nothing exemplified this ascetic attitude better than the work of the natural sciences. Transcending Biblical texts and ancient authorities, physics displayed a startling record of discovery through sheer observation and experiment. The ideological infrastructure of contemporary higher education is dominated then by science, discipline, and discovery.

The research mentality has much to recommend it–not least the astounding intellectual achievements of modern natural science. And if that is all there is or can be as ideological infrastructure in higher education, then it is clear why the nineteenth-century colleges with their dominant *moral* missions disappeared.

To understand the deep rationale of the older curriculum, one must contrast education for *discovery* with education for *recovery*. The modern research university operates on the core concept of *discovery*. Science is on an everlasting voyage of discovery. Methodological skepticism about present results projects Truth off into an unlimited future. This future-oriented research mentality of discovery is radically separated from the past-oriented "classical curriculum" of the denominational college. Education was not a road toward *discovery* but an exercise in *recovery*. Truth was already there in the Bible and some well-laundered Latins and Greeks. Thus Mark Hopkins's view that you only needed one book in the library.

Discovery is an exciting slogan, and I would not wish to lose its importance, but consider its fundamental limitations. I am more than content to wait out the fate of something called the high energy vector boson. Whether there are such, what they do, why they are important, may have to wait upon the abandoned Super Collider. If the bashful boson does not reveal itself in my lifetime, 'tis a pity, but let science forge on to its validated future. What I am not prepared to accept is that some ethical Einstein out there in the future will discover the real ethics, the perfect politics, and the meaning of life. When Immanuel Kant published his *Critique of Practical Reason* (on the nature of morality), a correspondent wrote congratulating him on the *discovery* of the moral law. The old philosopher was horrified and hurried to reply that he had not *discovered* the moral law—what had humanity been up to all those years! Kant suggested that he may have provided a new *formulation* of the moral law, but that was all.

The modern research university and its dominant paradigm study, natural science, may quite properly direct itself toward discovery. All well and good, but to the extent that *discovery* becomes its sole watchword, the university incapacitates itself for the tasks of ethics, aesthetics, politics, and religion. We really do think that morality and values in general are somehow *already*—not in every jot and tittle, but somehow and substantially *already at hand.* What is absurd is to believe that someday some successor of Kant will finally discover the moral law. *New York Times,* 1 January 2002: Philosophers in Pittsburgh Discover the Meaning of Life. Pope resigns. Dalai Lama refuses to answer telephone.

I am making no grand metaphysical claim to the effect that morality and meaning are somehow inherent in the mind, soul, or spirit. I only want to insist that morality and the meaning of life are not waiting to be invented like high-temperature superconductivity. Whatever the metaphysics of moral faculties, the fact is that morality in some sense already exists, maybe gathered together bit by bit from the ruminations of prophets, sages, men of action, women of sense—but there it is. Whatever the metaphysics, morality is *already.*

If morality is *already*, there are, however, two radically different interpretations of that view: that morality is recovered from past *history*, or revealed in *pure reason* above the historical facts of human behavior. Denominationalism opted for morality-from-the-past in the revelation of the Bible and the example of the Greeks. The whole trend of modern thought since the Enlightenment has been to reject the merely-historical, bringing the Bible, the Greeks, and any other cultural claimant under the judgment of Reason. I think that the historically-minded folks were correct. I offer in proof an encounter I once had in course on the philosophy of art.

At the beginning of the course, I asked all the students to indicate with which of the arts they were familiar: painting, ballet, music and so on. One student said that he had no acquaintance with any of the arts.

Why, then, was he taking this course? To get the general *theory* of art so that when he actually started to look at paintings and listen to music, he could discriminate the good stuff from the trash. The student was a true Enlightenment rationalist. If one knows the theory of art, then one can apply the theory to the actual instances. But this is not how it works. No prior "theory" of art such as my earnest student hoped for could direct the artist's work or inform the critic.

The rationalist wants a theory which transcends the historical instances. If values–moral, aesthetic, religious–are not *already* in transcendent reason, then to the universalist mind they come from Nowhere! If value is not grounded in Reason, it has no ground to stand on, it is a subjective attitude, passion, belief of individuals and groups without any universal warrant. The rationalist may gladly accept my "art" example, and conclude that morality is just so: a matter of taste and cultural bias. Contemporary multiculturalists may also agree with the rationalist that value is a function of specific histories. To the scientist of universal mind, so much the worse for values: they are among those subjective facts of human behavior, no more to be given universal credence than the odd behavior of some remote tribe should be taken as standard for the race. The multiculturalist may, in turn, be more than willing to accept this "subjectivizing" of value. There is *my* culture and mores which certainly are not *yours*.

What is lacking in the argument (or agreement) between the Rationalist and the deconstructionist is the importance of *tradition*. Values create traditions which in turn become standards subjecting particular revelations and enthusiasms to discipline, order and, one may say, "rationality," albeit not transcendent scientific Reason. To be reasonable is not necessarily to follow a deductive theory.

If "tradition" is the key to the rationality of values, it is important to recognize that the Protestant assumptions of the old sectarian colleges and the scientific assumptions of the research university have serious problems with the very idea of tradition. Both sectarians and rationalists can be staunchly anti-traditional, requiring whatever is historical to stand before the bar of better judgment. Protestants placed the Church tradition at the bar of the Bible, and found it wanting; rationalists put the Biblical tradition to the bar of science, and found it wanting. Both Bible and Reason transcend historical development in God's eternal word or Jeffersonian self-evident truths.

The old-style denominational college was correct in seeking value in a pedagogy of *recovery*–in *historical* recovery–but it froze history to the Biblical word of God and the immortal Greeks. That locates value *in* history, but it forbids development and discipline *through* history. Nevertheless, there is a deep lesson to be learned from the classical curriculum. In order to extract value from the former pedagogy, I turn to a modern curriculum which shadows the older style of teaching and does so with no apology: musical pedagogy.

Musical instruction retains the older pedagogy of repeated practice of classical masters leading to recital. Because music is a performing art we think this makes eminent good sense. The older college had paramount *moral* aims. Morality is also, in its own manner, a *performing* art. The moral purpose of the older colleges was well served by its repetitive exercises and required recital–not to mention all those rules, regulations, and revival meetings.

Consider the indispensable role of history and tradition in musical instruction. The important aspects of the music tradition–and of any genuine tradition–are *origin* and the *act of passing it on*. The origin is *historical*, rooted in a highly particular set of circumstances. A Beethoven symphony is a particular construction out of the historical existence of violins, woodwinds, and the like in the course of European music. Imagine trying to construct "the Symphony of Pure Reason" by transcending the contingency of instrumental availability, given styles of performance, and extant forms. One might get a concatenation of gamelan and oud, whistles and claps–anything. Music just is some contingent historical development of instruments, patterns, and sounds. There is no "pure theory of music," there is just the development from valued historical actualities; each "new" step is fitted into the tradition so that one can declare "That is music!" even though one had never heard such a crash and crescendo before.

The essential role of tradition in music explains why musical pedagogy follows the pattern of old-style denominational education. One imitates and recites from the tradition. The past tradition is a fixed repository of value to be conserved and passed on. Novelty and variation can only be assessed as they grow out of the past as a "rule" for the art. If the rationalist wants a Symphony of Pure Reason, the denominationalist acts as if music stopped with Bach! (For Lutherans maybe it did!)

In the course of the development of the musical tradition both in terms of learning to recite the tradition and expanding the tradition, there are various levels of reflection. One develops a "practical wisdom" for music, an ordered set of reflective comments about the underlying forms of music and the valuable expressive possibilities. "Novelties" occur: some are judged to be productive, others are clearly retrogressive. How do we know which? By trying to fit the practice alongside the actual achievements already before us. The "genius" who invents a new musical form or style of playing convinces us that it is as enriching as something already extant.

I want to emphasize that the musical scenario is *essentially historical* in contrast to the scientific "tradition." Science has a history of achievement. The critical difference is that science is genuinely *pro-*

gressive such that the truths of Newton are subsumed into the broader theories of relativity. Newtonian mechanics is fine at small scale, wrong at the cosmic level. Art, however, does not subsume its history. Cézanne said that he wanted to "redo Poussin in nature" but Poussin remains Poussin and irreplaceable even after Cézanne. Science continually incorporates its past into a present structure of theory; art preserves its past as the touchstone of its present and future. Science discards its past by incorporation; art keeps its past–and it is in this sense that in art values are "already."

I believe that, properly understood, education in and through a tradition is not only essentially historical but *essentially open minded.* Why is tradition essentially open minded? The short argument is clear from my musical example. In one sense music is Bach, Beethoven and the rest of the Bs. No one would think of training a musician except through grounding in the tradition, the classical canon. But, for all that, the modern composer does not repeat Bach–she will decide to "redo Bach in nature" and produce some cubist fugue for a Moog synthesizer. Tradition has the advantage of drawing on irreplaceable achievement; it has the disadvantage of always being only at "the state of the art."

I trust that you now comprehend the title of this lecture: "The Core Curriculum: It is Music to My Ears." While you may be caught in interminable wrangles down at the Arts College about what should be in the core, whether there is a core, why there is a core–the faculty over at your music school is happily drilling their students in the essential core of musical value and reflection. Of course the musical core gets tinkered with–sometimes significantly overhauled. But over time and with lots of careful listening, an open-textured core of music is established that no serious student of the art would reject whole and entire. The musical canon over time is like an extended family: the members of the canonic family are not identical, but one traces family resemblances across individuals in the set.

For education in the arts, the existence of a core, a canon of exemplary achievements, is essential. Harold Bloom needs his "strong poets" who can be overcome in Oedipal battle by the rising generation. The canon may be very rudimentary, but whenever whatever primitive tribe decided that the chief's little flute tune was worth passing along, the canon had commenced. Second flutist turns out to be second fiddle, and thus a standard of discrimination is established. Third flutist modulates into a minor key–and the musical tradition is on the road all the way to Milton Babbitt.

Can one expand the essential role of core or canon more generally across higher education? Yes and no. In establishing the importance of core curricula, we need to understand that there are "cores" and there are "cores"! If you have ever had to deal with ABET, the Accreditation

Board of Engineering and Technology, you would recognize that Electrical Engineering–to take one instance–is cored solid. At Rochester the students had *one* elective course in their four-year undergraduate program. One of the sheer political arguments for cores in the humanities and social sciences, is that our brethren in Engineering and the Natural Sciences seem to know exactly what you need to know to prosper in those areas, while the humanities often present a picture to the hapless student of helpless confusion.

But if there is to be a humanities core, it cannot follow the linear pattern of the Electrical Engineers. In order to understand the type of "core" appropriate for the humanities, I use a striking analogy from Wittgenstein. Wittgenstein pictures language as an ancient city. At the center of the city are twisted, winding streets. These streets grew up around the immediate, everyday life of people as they traded for food, constructed common governance, sought protection from nature and evil men, worshipped their gods. In modern times suburbs have grown up around the tangled network of center city. The suburbs have been laid out with rational precision, and have straight roads which expedite movement of men and material for efficient production and commerce. In the city of language, the suburbs are the natural sciences with their precise rules for classification, explanation, and demonstration. There is a studied "artificiality" about the suburban sciences which accounts for their power and effectiveness.

The center city of language, however, is the language of "everyday." It is not the world of quarks but the world of quirks–human quirks– which are as twisted and confusing as the ancient pathways. One of the fundamental curricular problems in higher education can be characterized as a quarrel between the suburbs and center city. Lots of folks have been mightily impressed with the clarity and power of the suburban road system, and have suggested it should be adopted throughout the linguistic domain. Anyone who decides that only science or some specially refined language is genuine will propose scientific urban renewal to straighten out the core streets of everyday talk. Center city talk–the chatter of the humanities–is unscientific, irrational. No wonder the humanities curriculum is a mess.

On the other hand, there are those who insist that, tangled as it may be, center city logic is non-replaceable, and that rational urban renewal will get you from one suburb to the next without passing through the delicately constructed heart of human experience. The challenge for those who insist on the irreplaceability of the central core of the city of language is how to guide the tourist through what seems at first nothing but a haphazard maze.

The core curriculum for center city cannot be like that established in the scientific suburbs. Travel in the suburbs is from point to point in a linear progression. One cannot get to quantum mechanics except by passing through calculus. The center city, in contrast, is explored by multiple criss-crossing from a myriad starting points to ever-varying destinations.

Why this difference between understanding in center city and the suburbs? I offer in brief the account based on Michael Oakeshott's analysis of human conduct.[1] Center city is the locus of rational agency. The "goings-on" in center city are something that humans have invented and thus the modes of behavior are as varied as the aims of the various inventions. Negotiating a contract is not the same as appraising a painting, is not the same as complaining to the telephone company, is not the same as etc., etc. Those who fancy scientific urban renewal imagine that all these varied activities can be ironed flat as examples of psychological stabilization, survival of the genes, the motion of molecules and so on all the way down from quirks to quarks.

The "goings-on" in center city as inventions are "learned" activities. The judge following civil law is not like the apple which falls following natural law. What is observed in center city are activities which the participants have had to learn to perform, from the humblest casual interchange to the loftiest pronouncements of the law. The assumption of our center city actions and talk is that there is an audience of other agents who understand special symbols and gestures, and are prepared to react to them as intelligent recipients of the messages offered. Because human practices are human inventions, their meaning must be *recovered* from traditions of practice, from customs of politeness to the proscribed duties of office. If center city is all human invention, what we invent we can change or abandon completely. It has seemed recently as if customs of politeness have been abandoned, to take one baleful example.

The problematic aspect of this focus on human *invention* is morality—and it is moral concerns that are the focal point of our contemporary quarrels about a core for higher education. Almost no one is likely to get greatly exercised about some canonic core of musical studies. If they do, it will be for moral, not musical reasons. We had a student at the Eastman School who refused to take a required course in medieval music because it was dominantly Christian music. Her objection was clearly moral, not musicological. There are two very different contemporary objections to morality in the core: multiculturalists object that it is the *wrong* morality; moral skeptics regard *any* moral core as lacking validity. Multiculturalists and moral skeptics may, however, reinforce one another in the curriculum committee. To the skeptic, no moral curriculum is any better than another, so one might as well indulge the aggrieved party.

Conservatives reject moral skepticism and regard multicultural "aestheticizing" of morality as a fundamental social disaster. Murder is wrong, just as two plus two equals four. There should be some surety for morality, or else it all drifts off to relativism. They are wary of morality as a "mere" invention.

The intuition about morality is correct but wrongly interpreted. The varied humanities of center city constitute the collection of distinctly human practices. Any and all of these practices are subject to radical change–even to abandonment. In music, opera is a relatively recent invention and one might conceive it being abandoned. What is not subject to radical change or total abandonment is morality. Oakeshott notes that morality is not a practice alongside other practices, it is the practice of practices. Morality is in a sense an *adverbial* characterization of specific practices, not itself a practice. As he says, it is not *killing* that is forbidden, it is *murderously* killing.[2] Whatever the specific center city practice, it rests on the assumption of interchange between rational agents; morality is the practice of practice, the dimensions and determinations of rational agency.

I commend Oakeshott's subtle analysis which I have barely stated, much less explicated or defended, but if one accepts the insight that morality is a language which qualifies substantive performances, the role of the "moral" core curriculum would be to teach facility in the use of this fundamental language of practice. I quote a wonderful passage from Oakeshott on this point:

[In moral language] there is room for the individual idiom...it may be spoken pedantically or loosely, slavishly or masterfully. Expressions in it harden into clichés and are released again; the ill educated speak it vulgarly, the purist inflexibly....The conduct of some is no better than an adventure in verbiage; clutching at imperfectly recollected and vaguely understood expressions...they are aware only of fashionable indignations....

With us, women are apt to speak this language differently from men; sometimes more and sometimes less punctiliously....They are apt to get along without a profound respect for rules and they are both more obstinate and more generous; when timid they are more servile and when courageous more reckless. The young speak it differently from the old, not merely because (as Aristotle remarks) they are less competent linguists, but because [of] what [one]...say[s] who

Drinks the valiant air of dawn

who is overwhelmed by the limitless invitations of human existence, and to whom 'the long littleness of life' is yet undreamed....Their ingenuousness is not wisdom, but in their shallow utterance a moral language may acquire a refreshing translucence....

Moral association is unavoidably concerned with the young and the old, with those setting out and those who are making the difficult exchange of hope for faith, with men and with women, with those who are born to die young and those who live into old age...each man hears and understands the promptings of some allegiances more clearly than others. As the ancient Greeks well knew, to honour Artemis might entail the neglect of Aphrodite.[3]

If you agree with this elegant characterization by Oakeshott, there are three useful lessons for the common curriculum.

First: morality is not itself a practice, it is a qualification of practices. As the inherent, inevitable accompaniment, it is teased out of everyday transactions. Morality is not something one faces onto as a distinct subject matter like law or music; one must catch it in the infrastructure of everyday practical discourse. It is like M. Jourdain's famous discovery that he was speaking *prose*; one does not go searching for morality, because it is omnipresent in all our actions. As Wittgenstein might have said, we lack "perspective" on ordinary language's inherent commitment to moral qualifications. Morality is something which we *re*cover because it has been there all along in all our practices.

Second lesson: it is clear that some people maneuver in moral language with great finesse and insight. And then there are moral pedants and moral purists who speak the language inflexibly. If our task is to educate our students in the adverbial world of morality, then we are obligated to place in the curriculum moral speakers of great subtlety and perception. That includes some or all of the usual suspects: Plato, Aristotle, Jane Austen, Tolstoy, and so on. It would be as absurd to deny these great moral speakers a preferred place in study as it would be to suggest that Mozart be dropped from the musical instruction. Given the problem of recovering what is, in a sense, right before us, the great moralists, as Socrates suggests, cause us to "reminisce."

Third lesson: for the multicultural urge–Oakeshott notes that the accents and emphases in moral discourse differ between men and women, the young and the old, those in pursuit of Artemis and those who are votaries of Aphrodite. We cannot learn all from each. The ingenuousness of the young is not wisdom, but in their shallow enthusiasm moral language may acquire a "refreshing translucence." Thus, although there are clearly masterpieces of moral language which any and all should learn to perform, all are colored by historical referent. The great Greek moral philosophers face onto the world of the *polis*, Jane Austen's exacting dissections of virtue are played out in the theater of her provincial home. We cannot transcend this historical color, and we can only learn about our own historical color through the perspective of an assortment of Greek aristocrats, English country ladies, and Russian nobility.

Constructing a core curriculum which is sensitive to morality requires a criss-crossing of thick, embedded, ever present moral vocabulary.

Those who want a frontal assault on morality end up as Oakeshott's pedants and purists aware at best of "fashionable indignations." Great moralists are greatly sensitive to the intricate fabric of moral deeds and discourse, and they deserve place in our studies. Finally, the core is necessarily open to those who are specially positioned by life, condition, and choice, since in this dense world of moral concern, they may not see all, but what they see, they see with special power.

Jacobsen was mistaken in his lawsuit. No college or curriculum can *deliver* wisdom. In one sense it cannot be delivered–or discovered–because it is already there, under our everyday discourse. In another sense, it cannot be delivered because it is so intricate and so interwoven with specific lives and practices. You may have to live a life in Rome or Paris or the center city of moral practice to understand the "habits of the heart," but it would be the better part of prudence to offer our best tour guides to visitors. I applaud the efforts of this Association to sustain that simple wisdom.

Sections of the above paper are adapted from Dennis O'Brien, All the Essential Half-Truths About Higher Education *(Chicago: University of Chicago Press, 1997). I am grateful to the Association for allowing me to share these ideas. The occasion offered me an opportunity to do what I did not do in the book: explore more fully the comparison and contrast between music (and the pedagogy of the arts in general) and the learning of moral languages: Oakeshott's "practice of practice."*

Notes
1. Michael Oakeshott, *On Human Conduct* (Oxford: Clarendon Press, 1975). See chapter 1, "On the Theoretical Understanding of Human Conduct." "Goings-on" is Oakeshott's term, a neutral designation for both natural process and human agency.
2. Oakeshott, 58.
3. Op. cit., 65-66.

The Belief Game

Stephen Zelnick

Temple University

I would like to launch into these remarks by reminding us of what we do and what our philosophy is. When I reviewed the notes I made last night from Louise Cowan's address, I realized she has done that very well. So permit me to review points from her speech because it expresses so well what ACTC is about and leads into the subject of my talk.

Dr. Cowan noted that one principle objective is to study seriously a wide variety of texts. I brought with me a list of the texts that we cover in Temple's Intellectual Heritage Program, and I suspect it is similar to many other programs in ACTC. The list is frankly outrageous. We study a wide variety of texts, across many disciplines and many cultures. We teach twelve texts in fourteen weeks, simple texts, like *The Republic* and *Antigone*, texts that just sort of teach themselves. And we teach these texts to students who are not very good readers yet and have not thought all that much about the world. That is what we do.

As Louise points out, we believe that liberal knowledge is founded in communities where all students read the same books. We don't teach students one at a time. We teach them in classes, we engage their different disciplinary interests, and we open a discussion we want them to participate in most vitally.

We provide a common foundation. At Temple, every student who graduates has had to sit and read Locke's *Second Treatise of Government* and suffer through those long sentences that threaten never to come to a conclusion and those abstractions, page after page without an example, and finally work hard to make some connection between this strange seventeenth-century lawyer's treatise and the world they live in. Every one of our students has been through the baptism of fire, and come through it with an appreciation for a philosophy that is deeply embedded in the way we think about ourselves and our most important documents.

What we do means that every teacher of senior classes can say to a class, "Now, as Locke says in regard to the sources of property," or, "as you are aware in the tradition of Natural Rights philosophy..." and expect that the students will for the most part understand what that means. The notion of a curriculum that builds upon itself is simply what a curriculum is. It cannot be one course at a time, but it is a patterned and organized course of study. At Temple and in most ACTC schools, we read and study as a community, even when that community may be seventeen thousand students, as is the case at Temple University.

Nor is it the case that we satisfy ourselves with excerpted snippets. Students should be reading whole texts. In IH, even despite the daunting list, for as much as we can, we read whole texts. Doing so retains the integrity of the texts and allows the student's imagination to bloom inside the whole structure of a texts, whereas snippets seems so peculiar. What is a student to do with a snippet?

The classics of Western Civilization need to figure prominently, though not exclusively, Dr. Cowan advises. We have a legacy of texts— it is Homer, Plato, Sophocles, the Bible, Shakespeare and so on. These are powerful and literally wonderful texts, and texts that everyone who wishes to enter the larger discussion throughout time and across the world needs to know. We think our students need to know the adjective "Machiavellian." You can't read the newspaper without knowing that, and you can't know what the adjective is really about without reading *The Prince*. Without being familiar with the Hebrew Bible and the Gospels, to those who have not encountered the powerful poetry of the New Testament much of the language that swirls around us is strange. Our courses cannot be made up of titles willy-nilly but of books that matter and that form the web and woof of our language and conversation.

Finally, Dr. Cowan also advises that we make an effort to evoke belief—and that is the subject of my talk today. We need to be speaking that famous phrase—"you must change your life." Students do need to believe things and they find themselves very often in a crisis of belief, as we all tend to be. For many of our youth, the world around them does not sustain a structure that traditionally people have depended upon to structure their lives and a coherent version of themselves. Most of us have found a way to build such a structure, but these courses offer an extraordinary opportunity to provide that help to our students.

The sanctity of the text is one thing, but what goes on in the minds of our students is where everything is alive and real. This is the delivery point of everything we do. We need to enter our students' lives imaginatively, think about what they think, and listen to their voices with the same kind of intensity that we use to analyze these texts to understand the drama going on inside our students in their budding life. We need to understand that and, then, fashion a contact point between the texts we teach and those concerns. All that is involved with our perspective on learning. What will students take away from what we do? That has to be our perspective all the time. So, how do we do enter our students' lives and give them something to walk away with?

I want today to talk about the "Belief Game," as we call it in our program. Looking at the list I have distributed, you see the list of texts and you will notice that they do not all line up easily with one another. Several of them, in fact, are aimed at one another's vitals. The second problem we face is the readiness of students to reject everything. We read the Declaration of Independence–well, we know that Jefferson owned slaves, so much for the Declaration of Independence and its formulation of liberty and dignity of persons. John Locke owned shares for twenty-two months in the Royal Africa Company, so much for Locke's discussion of rights and freedoms. And on and on. There is no text or author that cannot be overwhelmed by some nasty story; whether it is right- or left-wing or anti-feminist, no text can stand against the scrutiny of moral perfection and absolute integrity.

To accommodate both these matters–the conflict between the texts, and the tendency in students to reject the authority of any text–I have installed what I call the Belief Game with my students. It works like this. Each text that we study, we are going to believe in absolutely. We are going to find every good reason to support it. We are going to find examples that are positive. We are going to take the text out into the world, and we're going to read the newspaper and observe the world around us in a way the confirms and sustains the argument being made in that text. So, when we read John Locke's *Second Treatise of Government*, for two weeks or more, we are going to be Lockeans. We are going to live inside the argument for independent and individual industriousness and rationality. We will become supporters of the notions of private property. We will become supporters of the most radical notions of liberty and natural rights. We will fashion arguments against our own government and its taxing structure–a lively topic in April–that takes away private wealth from an industrious person and redistributes it to persons who have perhaps not been industrious but fanciful and contentious instead. We will look at the family as Locke looks at it and discuss the roles and obligations of parents and children just as Locke does. And we will use Locke to constitute, at the beginning of our semester, the classroom as a polity with laws and rules. We will have a discussion and reach consent. We all agree to abide by rules that we have made together and to which we have given our consent. We may even sign formally some Magna Carta of the classroom to indicate our free and open consent that follows a free and open discussion that is not the result of force or violence, which we often discover has been the case in previous schooling. We will establish a John Locke classroom. For two of three weeks, we will be John Locke utterly. We are going to believe in reason–and see where it takes us. We will find examples in our newspapers to support and sustain Locke's argument. Then, we will read the Bill of Rights, the Declaration of Independence, and Frederick Douglass. We will immerse ourselves in this point of view–and not a peep out of you of resistance or objections!

Because it is a game–the Belief Game. The point of the game is to see where it takes us, to see what it feels like, to see what we become when we live in the midst of this text. There is, of course, something silly about this approach. It is a game, but games have powerful import. Just play one for a few minutes. My daughter likes to drag us out to go bowling. What a silly game, but when my wife is three pins ahead, I go berserk. Games have irresistible power. So we play the Belief Game.

You might well object. Students must develop a critical perspective. It just won't do to have students accept these books uncritically. Not a problem. Because after a short stay with John Locke and the Natural Rights tradition, we are all going to become Wordsworthians. We will look right through the assertions of individual, commercial endeavor, those bland surfaces that block out the more powerful, alienated real self that needs to be recovered and restored through the imagination. We need to recover a bond with nature that is not proprietary, not built on producing from nature to get wealth and things, but instead to find in nature an image of our finer selves, an image that supports a good man's life. That image should help us make intelligible again that unintelligible world that has become our life in the fret and fume of our busy life. And suddenly, Locke is tipped over a bit when we enter the world of Wordsworth.

We will have a stroll down that open road with Grandpa Whitman for several days. We will be ridiculous and outrageous and learn how important it is to become fanciful and contentious and not industrious and not rational and not acquisitive and proprietary. And to be antic and outrageous in discovering wild and free about ourselves, free in a way that Locke had not imagined. And we will be Whitman without limit and without boundary. We will be in the tradition of Whitman and Kerouac, and Ginsberg, Bob Dylan, and Pablo Neruda; for a while we are going to try to be the nuts that sing the song of workers and the body electric, at least in a way that will not embarrass us.

A week after that we will change our view; now we become communists. I warn them not to tell anybody! Strangely, at first, Karl Marx looks like Locke again. There's the labor theory of value, those who work keep the wealth they produce just as Locke said–but oh what a difference! We will establish solidarity with those who have been beaten down by history, those who have suffered and live in the misery of beastly labor without hope. We find instances, without difficulty, in our world local and global. We talk about how Nike shoes are manufactured and what happens to young women in East Asia as a consequence of capitalist practices. We will have a look at those sneakers the students are wearing to class and talk about the implications of the circuitry of capitalism. We are going to talk about unions in the history of this country and the experiences of their grandparents and previous generations struggling for economic rights. We will have a look at our neighborhoods and think about how to redistribute labor and wealth, and how to imagine, beyond a revolution, how to build a world that would not be one of beastly labor and compulsion and a vast gap of wealth and power between people, a world instead of dignity for every individual, one where not state is needed to compel you, a world of communities that rule themselves.

But not to worry. We will be doing Freud soon enough, and he will explain why all of Locke and Marx are impossible, if not ridiculous, because human beings would never stand for anything so rational and orderly. And on and on–you see how it goes throughout the semester. At each stage what is required is absolute commitment to the project of that particular text.

Of course we need to observe with care how each text supports itself. What are the warrants and claims? How are the arguments for each position constructed? What evidence gives them power? In fact, I posted a message this morning to my students who I abandoned so I could speak to you. I asked them to observe Freud's remark that "man is a wolf to man" in *Civilization and its Discontents*. I asked them, "What argument would you bring forward to support such a claim, and having done so what convinces you this claim is valid?" This question will come at us again in our meeting with Gandhi, who makes a very different claim about humanity. And there we will do our best to be Gandhians based on strong arguments, evidence, proofs. In this regard, the Belief Game keeps us close to the efforts to find strong reasons.

It is true that the Belief Game tends to waste opportunities to find contradictions in the text as you are studying it. But you gain the belief structure. If we had time enough, we might do the entire course again from the negative perspective. What are all the reasons for rejecting Locke's argument? We might settle the difference by doing both, but what is lost is the opportunity to engage a belief, more or less fully, to walk around in the world for even a week inside that set of notions to see where it takes you and what it feels like. Look, my students are all too ready with their criticisms, so much so that the other opportunity for living in someone else's beliefs will not arise by itself. For this reason, I have gone in the direction of belief.

Another obvious objection to this parade of commitments is that it will lead to utter relativism and leave the student with no structure of belief to depend upon. It often seems to me that real relativism is based on a notion that there are no sustaining belief systems at all. And that's not what this design assumes. Instead, students will have experienced in the course six or eight different structures of belief in some vital way. Then, they have the rest of their education and lives to shop amongst these various beliefs or to cobble together one of their own out of the experience of them; but for two weeks they will be living Locke utterly.

Yet, in my game I am never allowed to tell what I personally believe. It is my job to believe each one of these authors. And the funny thing is, I do. These pursuits of truth are part of my inner discussion. However, it is unfair for me to say to the students, "this is what I really believe," for that forecloses several of the positions along the way. Student will ask me when we are two-thirds into the course, "well, what do you believe?" And my answer is, that shouldn't be of interest to you. I wouldn't want to proscribe your discovery of what is true for you by asking you to accept the authority of whatever I have concluded. First off, I could be wrong. Second, the point is for you to build for yourself what proves to be true for you and your experience.

To be sure, something is lost in that response because traditionally teachers are to be exemplars of something, and in the game I play I have to bracket that commitment. But, the fact is, you cannot give someone the truth. Once upon a time, when I was younger and knew better, when I knew the truth, I used to teach students what they should believe, and the result was embarrassingly awful. I would never do that or recommend anyone to do that. It's a dreadful error. And it is unfair and undemocratic because you are an adult with power over them, and the point is to get each one of us to take the long journey and not to pick them up in a limo and drive them to the final destination.

Instead, if you play the belief game, the students will have done something else that is important to ACTC. They will have entered the discussion. That is our tradition, a tradition of discussion and debate; a tradition of disputation, where a voice speaks, you reply, my counter example follows; a tradition where we battle it out through reason within our community to find out what is most true for us; a tradition where we try to persuade each other and, who knows, in the process may learn something and be convinced of something we had felt strongly against. This is a more precious lesson for our students about a vital and democratic community than they have ever imagined. The Belief Game belongs to what we are all about.

Principles

Lost Worlds:

Beyond Piety to New Beginnings in *The Aeneid*

Peter C. Brown

Mercer University

> ...it is the gods' relentlessness, the gods', that overturns these riches....
> Virgil, *The Aeneid* (Mandelbaum 2.815-16)

The Latin poet Virgil was acutely aware of the interplay of tradition and innovation. His great poem, *The Aeneid*, strove to create a heroic and divine tradition for the new Augustan Rome. At the same time, his epic parodied the narratives of Homer's much earlier epics. But, these narrative continuities and discontinuities, interesting as they may be, are the narrow province of historians and classicists. The larger *interdisciplinary* interest of *The Aeneid* lies in the way Virgil's text frames the general and, for us, highly relevant question, "How do we preserve that which has been lost?" This is the literal issue of Aeneas' fugitive voyagings and trials at arms: how to preserve the Trojan line from its conclusive disaster? It is also the general spiritual dilemma of any age of transition. *The Aeneid* addresses an audience caught between worlds, between an irretrievable past and a dimly perceived, if hopeful, future. Thus, as Allen Mandelbaum insists, there is something both autumnal and utopian in Virgil's voice, something triumphant yet pastoral.

We too live in an age of transition ("modernity" might be defined as living in perpetual transition). But, in contrast to Virgil, we seem too often either resigned or resentful as we contemplate cultural changes that appear inevitable and yet unpredictable. The revolutionary engine of modern capitalism with its technological innovations thrusts us into an unknown future, while the agonies of conflict in this century have undermined the faith in social and moral progress that once justified the ways of history to us. We tend neither any longer to look to the past for its glories nor to the future for its promises. And the present state of textual criticism in the humanities seems often to mirror this unhappy collapse of both tradition and innovation into suspicion and cynicism, into an irony that often feels–to many of us and to many of our students–like a cop-out. We live in a time badly in need of hope and new beginnings. Virgil's *Aeneid* not only addresses this problem with vital insight, but as a classic text it offers us a particularly convincing example of the potential of interdisciplinary core texts to reconnect us to our past in a way that renews and tutors our appetite for the future.

Within the first fifty lines of *The Aeneid*, Virgil's narrator raises the question why "It was so hard to found the race of Rome" (1.50)? Juno's enmity, pestilence, storm, and revolt, and the hardy opposition of Turnus and his troops are but outward signs of an inward dilemma that profoundly baffles Aeneas' attempts to begin life anew for his Trojan remnant. The essential nature of his confusion emerges as he tells Queen Dido the tale of Troy's fall. Again and again on that terrible night, he was drawn to desperate battle, and again and again he was turned aside from combat and toward his home and family. His warrior's virtues, the identity of a lifetime, must be discarded in favor of the domestic virtue of piety: reverence for his patrimony. In contrast to Hector in *The Iliad*, he attempts to save his father's house by fleeing the battlefield–his crippled father upon his back. Paradoxically, faithfulness requires transformation; we honor our precedents only when we ourselves are capable of profound change.

This paradox is deepened as Aeneas reluctantly sails away from Dido's Carthage–a fair landing indeed. Faithfulness requires something more than safe haven and self-preservation. Indeed, it will require the unthinkable, that Aeneas resign his characteristic virtue–his hardily won piety! He must cease to be reactive, defensive, oriented to his past. He must know himself as father, as well as, as son. The shade of his father, Anchises, releases him from his retrospective homage and turns him toward the novel fate he must forge for his son and his son's sons. It is an incalculable gift for our past to allow us to relinquish it with no taint of betrayal. But, as Aeneas teaches us, it still requires a wrenching personal commitment to exile. As the concerted gods insist, "Troy now is fallen; let her name fall, too" (12.1100). To preserve Troy is finally to merge Troy in a new identity, to begin a new history and tradition. In vital change is continuity *and* renewal–but at an unfathomable price for pious souls.

Virgil's epic is a meditation on the nature of human time and, as such, already stands within a very ancient tradition stretching back to Gilgamesh and his cry: "Let something remain of all I love." Virgil brings to this tradition the long view of history. He brings a sharpened sense of the rise and flourishing and crisis and transformation of cultural heritage, a perspective that is perhaps not matched again until modernity. He knew he stood at a transitional moment in his own political and cultural heritage (he was Celtic as well as Roman!). He knew–or imagined–that others had stood at such moments before him and that others *would* stand at such moments after him. Aeneas' energized bewilderment in the underworld as the shade of his father shows him the swarming spirits of his posterity is one of our most suggestive cultural figures for the imaginative jump that must connect a lost past to an uncreated future. Virgil realizes that a creative future can arise within a painful breech of time's continuity, a breech within which we must honor what we cannot live out. In *The Aeneid*, vital innovation occurs through a temporal bewilderment that can be motivated through continuity toward change. Aeneas' unknowable Latin destiny has its unlikely birth in his devotion to his father as the towers of Ilium tumble about them.

The Aeneid is now, of course, part of our own, long lost past; we, reading Virgil, have an even more acute sense of cultural transition than he did. The civilization whose triumph he celebrates has undergone its unimaginable sea changes, become a legendary Troy itself. But Virgil's insight into the sources of hope for pious souls caught in such moments of transition is still as fresh as ever. If, on the one hand, we see our traditions as something to preserve and as something that, in turn, preserves us, then we are sadly doomed to desperate flight from reality and ultimate defeat. The gods *are* truly relentless–in the reaches of human time, all our riches will be overturned. If, on the other hand, we see our traditions (and they are deeply plural) as embodying the vital ancestral impulses of the human race, we are free to appreciate and appropriate these impulses for our own moment, our own futures, our own posterity. To paraphrase the American cultural critic F. O. Matthiessen, every great civilization must create its own tradition out of whatever in the past enables it to transcend itself. The future *is* our only hope, but that future's best prospects lie in a *transformative* faithfulness, a faithfulness beyond piety–a faithfulness that demands profoundly new beginnings.

We live in a time of great sophistication and extraordinarily rapid social change; it may seem that we have transcended any fixed points of reference from our cultural legacies. Certainly, there is no going back; reaction is understandable, fruitless, and inherently coercive. But we have also lost much of our confidence in our ability to go forward. The classic texts of our traditions each embody moments of powerful cultural innovation, whether of pure novelty, greater coherence, or deeper criticism. They expand the range of meaning for their times. They help create the future that is our past. Unless we can share that innovative impulse and grasp the human complexities upon which it operates, we are condemned to live at the thin edge of the present, in mere flux. What Virgil (Gilgamesh, Jeremiah, Socrates, Dante, Cervantes, etc., etc.) teach us is that we all, always, live in flux *but* that we also have the capacity again and again to shape the meaning of our time, even if only perhaps to express for the moment our regret and sense of abandonment. Without this connection to living tradition, how can we prevent our future being just one damned thing after another?

Do we stand where Virgil stood? We necessarily lack the retrospect to know the nature of our transitional cultural moment, but, in another sense, we obviously stand with him expressing our hopes and fears, reading the runes and ruins of our time, shaping our and our posterity's futures. Our students need to understand this and need to learn how to join this company of bewildered visionaries. There is no better way, I believe, to accomplish this than by a faithful and "impious" reading of our classic progenitors—our inspirations, not our guides. Our traditions do *not* contain the answers *we* need; we must forge anew our own responses to our times. But our traditions *do* contain the humane questions and vital imagination that we must be able to appropriate if we are to rise worthily to the challenges of human living in our moment. Our highest calling is to help our students to this appropriation.

Works Cited

Mandelbaum, Allen, trans. *The Aeneid of Virgil*. New York: Bantam, 1971.
Matthiessen, F.O. *American Renaissance*. New York: Oxford University Press, 1941.

A "Red-Tory" Feminist, at Core

Peggy Heller

University of King's College

And new Philosophy cals all in doubt,
the Element of fire is quite put out;...
'Tis all in pieces, all cohaerence gone;
All just supply, and all Relation[1]

There are many who evidently consider that this is a just description
of the present state of higher education. As we near the end of the mil-
lennium some believe that learning itself is coming to an end. Harold
Bloom in his *Western Canon* echoes the sense of foreboding of Yeats'
poem, "The Second Coming": "things have however fallen apart, the
center has not held, and mere anarchy is in the process of being un-
leashed upon what used to be called 'the learned world.'"[2] The glue
that had held this world together has been corroded by the passionate
intensity of the worst, of which feminists are key members. Such a tone
of lament is common to a number of what I'll call conservative commentators, in a number of works with which we are all familiar.[3] For
these, the re-assertion of the benefits of a curriculum of core texts is the
action of a valiant rearguard keeping Western civilization safe from the
paynim. The traditional core curriculum guards the core of ideas concerning what we are, at core, as human beings. Feminism is an enemy,
acting to dissolve, destroy, deconstruct, demolish.

And there are feminists who agree with this. "For anti-feminists,
feminism corrupts the academy; for some feminists, the academy cor-

rupts feminism" writes Diane Elam. According to certain feminists, the western canon is essentially phallocentrism, a monolithic weapon of domination, to put it politely. Such a feminist view is found, for example, in an extreme form in the works of Mary Daly, who wrote in her *Gyn/Ecology*: "We have seen that the deadly perpetrators of this planetary atrocity are acting out the deadly myths of patriarchy and that ritual enactment of the sado-myths has become more refined with the 'progress of civilization.'" More typically, feminists such as Susan Moller Okin in her *Women in Western Political Thought* and Denise Riley in her *"Am I that Name?"*[4] approach the core texts through a sustained critique of the treatment of women in Western philosophy. The core of texts, although still considered by them to be an inheritance, is no longer thought of as a precious family jewel to be preserved throughout the ages but more as a legacy carrying with it the family curse.

Both ways of imaging the coreness of core texts, that is as a precious pearl or accursed monolith, are problematic. The conservative commentators should attend to the warning of Heidegger in "The Age of the World-Picture": "The flight into tradition, out of a combination of humility and presumption, can bring about in itself no other than self-deception and blindness in relation to the historical moment."[5] On the other hand, those feminists in flight away from tradition blind themselves to the extent to which their own critical stances and their own aspirations are beholden to what used to be called the great books. That is not to say that women's relation to what is largely a patrimony can be a simple one, as I'll get to in a moment.

It is instructive that the stances both of traditionalism and of critique do not seek any dialogue with each other in search for reconciliation but have been content rather to assert themselves in mutual opposition. This alerts us to what I believe is the essentially Nietzschean character of both of them. In *On the advantage and disadvantage of history for life*,[6] Nietzsche sought to oppose the deadening effects of an academic approach to history which modeled itself upon science by claiming that the study of history should only be undertaken if it can engage the student as did myth. The three animating and therefore good reasons for looking to the past (and I'm subjecting this to a certain amount of creative interpretation) are to find in it a source of great exemplars, to provide oneself with aesthetic pleasure, and to affirm present values by repudiating former beliefs and practices. I suggest that the conservative commentators promote a curriculum based on core texts from the first two motivations and the feminist commentators critique such an enterprise from the third.

Nietzsche was right, I think, to oppose himself to the kind of scientific objectification of historical knowledge in which the human past stands apart as a detached object from the human subject. It is, after all, to overcome such detachment of the knower from the known that we here try to overstep the structures of the modern university and teach the way we do. Yet in his saving of the subject or the knower, the object or what is to be known is lost altogether. Nietzschean appropriations of the past fail to free us from the confines of our own constructions: they can therefore never educate, for education involves being led outside oneself. It is no wonder that arguments between traditionalists and anti-traditionalists in the various canon debates have been so angry, for if argument is nothing other than the agonistics of self-assertion there is no common ground to refer to for resolution. But struggle for domination is in the end neither productive, nor interesting, nor instructive. You can't will a core, for what is central must have its own weight. I want to make a proposal for how to get out of what I think is a Nietzschean dead end. If we are to approach the past in Nietzsche's modes of monumental history, antiquarian history and critical history, the moments of reverence, appreciation, and critique are separated and even opposed. Such separation and opposition of the moments of the human soul are *hell*, according to Dante. If we reconsider them as inter-related, we come up with something like the Augustinian moments of the soul: memory, love, and reason. And, if we re-evaluate our fundamental motivations in this way, we will understand why we should study and teach the core texts: to bring to light the roots of what we are through memory, to enjoy what is wonderful through love, and to analyze what can be understood through reason. Having brought memory, desire, and intellect into relation, we discover that we are neither simply conservatives nor simply critics but what I am calling, not in a vein of seriousness, "red-Tories." My model here is J. S. Mill at the stage in his life when he was trying to hold together the ideas of Coleridge, who thought that societies required "some fixed point; something which men agree in holding sacred" (a core, in other words), with those of Bentham, who thought that all institutions must be brought to the bar of judgment by reason.[7] The red-Tory wants it all: gratitude for inherited traditions and hope for a more just future. The red-Tory is both conservative and progressive. The red-Tory approaches the core texts with attitudes both of critical reverence and reverent criticism. The red-Tory feels beholden to the past without idolizing it, is critical without being destructive.

Now that I have attempted to reinstate a pre-Enlightenment understanding of the soul and with it an un-Nietzschean approach to the past, I want to show why we still need to be feminists in our approach to the core texts, however reverential that approach may be. My example will be a text that I assume most here would agree belongs in a core curriculum, indeed most would agree is a "great book," Dante's *Divine*

Comedy. The feminist critique of this work that might be anticipated is that Dante did not present Beatrice as a full human being standing on her own, as it were, but as a figure of the eternal feminine, constructed out of the desires of a masculine self. For Simone de Beauvoir, the presentation of Beatrice is yet another example of men finding in Woman the embodiment of their ideals as she is for them but "the material representation of alterity."[8] In a fascinating twist of fate, Harold Bloom understands Beatrice in exactly the same way: "Dante," Bloom writes, "like Petrarch falls in love with his own creation. What else could Beatrice be?"[9] Yet I must say I agree with Dorothy Sayers' judgment that if this is what we expect Beatrice to be, she in her actual presence in the poem will shock us by being surprisingly individual and disturbingly vocal.[10] The character Dante is not allowed by the poet Dante to treat Beatrice as embodied wish-fulfillment. Dante warns himself and his readers of the sin of investing others with what we project onto them through the dream of the Siren.

No, my questioning of Dante is not a complaint concerning his unfair treatment of the female characters, nor about him being "sexist." Rather, I question Dante in the light of the demand, which is a contemporary demand, that the subjectivity of women be represented when human subjectivity as such is represented. Put in another way, women no longer accept the burden alone of adjustment to the universal "man" when such a universal contradicts, denies or deprecates what they are. As I, being a woman, attempt to follow Dante on his journey allegorized as the journey of the soul of everyman, meaning every person, I encounter in certain levels of interpretation barriers to my own identification with that journey. Especially in the allegory of romantic love, desire as such is patterned only on male desire. If one tries in imagination to reverse the roles of Dante and Beatrice, and to suppose that it is Beatrice undertaking the journey toward Dante, it will not work. The Lady is the object of the quest, not the one who quests. Beatrice is indeed portrayed as a living and rational individual, yet what moves her is not represented. Her heart is unknown. Gerda Lerner argues that even the medieval female mystics did not represent female desire in their writings: "they lack precisely the activity and assertiveness whereby the self becomes an exemplar of the life leading to salvation. The female mystics rather submerged the self in order to become open to ecstatic revelations."[11] But in our own time, as women have become subjects speaking their own memories and aspirations, a new demand is being placed on the older understandings of what it is to be human. The journey of the fully human soul has yet to be told: Dante's portrayal, despite its scope, is partial for it does not include what a woman is for herself. The contemporary reading of core texts cannot avoid being a feminist one (but not that alone) because the texts need to answer why they have proposed accounts of universal humanity which have failed to be so. It is a mark of our respect that we do not allow the great books to be excused by the conventions of the times in which they were written, conventions which in other respects they themselves freely questioned.

I began with John Donne's mourning for a coherence he thought had been forever lost. From our vantage point we can see Descartes coming over the horizon and the establishment of modernity. Whatever faults we may discern in the Age of Reason, incoherence was not among them. Likewise in our own century it appears to some that things are falling apart, that there is no center, that the past is no more for us than a heap of broken images. But I sense rather that this is a time of transition to a greater coherence, in which what used to be excluded can now be brought into relation. I sense, with the Swiss poet Philippe Jaccottet, that the possibility is given to us in this time to "speak more rigorously true than ever, in conformity with what we are."[12] I want to end, therefore, with a re-imaging of the image of a core. The soul was likened by Plato in *The Republic* to the sea-god Glaucus, whose beauty was obscured by encrustation of shells, seaweeds and rocks.[13] The task of philosophy is to free the soul so that it can be seen in all its beauty. This image of the soul could certainly also be one kind of image that the term "core" invokes: a core is like a beautiful pearl, self-complete and perfect, needing to be preserved from corruption, contamination and obscurity. For critics of the traditional core curriculum, the image that "core" suggests on the contrary is that of a patriarchal monolith. But we red-Tories may imagine the core rather as being something alive and perhaps sponge-like which, when new waters wash around it, bringing with them strange life-forms, undergoes a sea-change: it remains both itself and yet takes on a different hue. Perhaps we should think of the core not as a polished jewel, nor as a blunt instrument, but as something squishy.

Notes

1. John Donne, *The First Anniversarie: An Anatomy of the World* [1611], facsimile reprint of the 1621 edition (London: Noel Douglas, 1926), 205-6, 213-14.

2. Harold Bloom, *The Western Canon: the Books and School of the Ages* (New York: Harcourt Brace, 1994), 1.

3. Among many others, Allan Bloom, *The Closing of the American Mind* (New York: Simon and Schuster, 1987); Dinesh D'Souza, *Illiberal Education: the Politics of Race and Sex on Campus* (New York: Free Press, 1991); Arthur M. Schlesinger, Jr., *The Disuniting of America: Reflections on a Multicultural Society* (New York: Norton, 1992).

4. Diane Elam, *Feminism and Deconstruction: Ms. en Abyme* (London: Routledge, 1994), 92; Mary Daly, *Gyn/Ecology: the Meta-ethics of Radical*

Feminism (Boston: Beacon Press, 1978), 315; Susan Moller Okin, *Women in Western Political Thought* (Princeton: Princeton University Press, 1979); and Denise Riley, *"Am I that Name?"*: *Feminism and the Category of "Women" in History* (Minneapolis: University of Minnesota Press, 1988).

5. Martin Heidegger, "The Age of the World Picture" in *The Question Concerning Technology and Other Essays*, trans. William Lovitt (New York: Harper and Row, 1977), 136.

6. Translated as *The Use and Abuse of History*, trans. Adrian Collins, Library of Liberal Arts (Indianapolis: Bobbs-Merrill, 1949).

7. *Mill on Bentham and Coleridge*, with an Introduction by F. R. Leavis (Cambridge: Cambridge University Press, 1980), 123.

8. Simone de Beauvoir, *The Second Sex*, trans. and ed. H. M. Pashley, with an Introduction by Deirdre Bair (New York: Vintage, 1989), 179.

9. *Western Canon*, 103.

10. Dorothy Sayers, introduction to *The Divine Comedy 2: Purgatory* (Harmondsworth, Eng.: Penguin, 1955), 25-44.

11. Gerda Lerner, *The Creation of Feminist Consciousness: from the Middle Ages to Eighteen-seventy* (New York: Oxford University Press, 1993), 47.

12. Philippe Jaccottet, "Observations (fragment)" in *Crystal and Smoke*, trans. Michael Bishop (Wolfville, N.S.: Editions du Grand Pres), forthcoming.

13. *Republic*, 611d.

Method

Aristotle and the Distinction of Disciplines

Montague Brown

Saint Anselm College

This paper will be rather more about tradition than innovation, although the tradition it invokes suggests that a "core text" or "great books" program can do much to renew the human spirit in our age of specialization. One of the problems with a "great books" approach is that the unity of the course may not be apparent. This is not surprising, since the texts studied are often from quite different disciplines. One way of trying to tie everything together is to emphasize a theme throughout the course. Quite often this will be an ethical theme, which will tend to work pretty well, since one can raise about any work the question of the motivation of the author or of the characters within the work. The danger in such a course is that the essential elements of the distinct disciplines may be lost. While this mix of disciplines runs the risk of confusion and thematic limitation, in the end this multidisciplinary nature of a "core text" or "great books" program is one of its great strengths.

The paper will have three parts. In the first, the problem of course unity will be raised in reference to the diverse texts typical of a Great Books Seminar. In the second, Aristotle's reasons for not blurring distinctions between disciplines will be discussed, with special reference to his thought in the *Poetics*. Finally, reasons will be given for why the multidisciplinary nature of such a course is a real strength.

Consider the following list of texts, which is quite typical of the range of materials found within a Great Books Seminar in the Liberal Studies Program at Saint Anselm College: Homer's *Odyssey*, Plato's *Republic*, *History of the Peloponnesian War* by Thucydides, *The Agamemnon*, *Libation Bearers*, and *Eumenides* by Aeschylus, *Oedipus the King*, *Oedipus at Colonus*, and *Antigone* by Sophocles, *Medea* and *Heracles* by Euripides, Aristophanes' *The Clouds* and *The Birds*, Aristotle's *Poetics* and other selections from his writings, and historical portraits of Pericles, Alcibiades, Solon, and Themistocles by Plutarch. Here we have not only three different major groupings—literature, philosophy and history—but also differences within these three areas. In the area of literature, epic, tragedy, and comedy are studied. In reading Plato's *Republic* and the selections from Aristotle, the students face questions of ethics, politics, logic, human nature, metaphysics, and aesthetics. As for history, the approaches of Thucydides and Plutarch are quite different. It is not easy to move between such disciplines on an almost daily basis.

In the attempt to make connections between the texts, one may choose to emphasize ethical or political themes, or perhaps focus on human nature or on the history behind the texts. All of these threads are interesting and worthwhile in themselves, but they tend to dominate texts in ways that do violence to what is most central to the texts. For example, to try to explain Plato's philosophical positions in *The Republic* by referring to the historical conditions under which he wrote, or to try to draw a moral lesson from *The Odyssey*, or to take Aristophanes' portrayal of Socrates in *The Clouds* as historically true is to miss the main point of each text. Plato is arguing for positions which transcend time; Homer is not an ethical philosopher; and *The Clouds* is a comedy, whose first purpose is to entertain.

Aristotle is famous for his insistence that different disciplines have different principles and require different methods. Since mathematics, biology, physics, metaphysics, ethics, and aesthetics are about different subject matters, one would do violence to them by treating them all under one method. For the purpose of this paper, I shall be drawing on Aristotle's treatment of this important point in the *Poetics*. Thus, my remarks will be apropos most directly of how one ought (and ought not) to treat literature. However, the same general point about focusing on what is essential is applicable to studying any work.

While the *Poetics* deals mostly with tragedy, Aristotle has quite a bit to say about epic and a little about comedy. Thus, although the work is not very specific about what makes for good painting or good architecture or good music, it is quite suitable for a discussion of literature (apart, perhaps, from the short lyric poem). When speaking of art in general, Aristotle says that there are two reasons why we enjoy making and appreciating art: "imitating is innate in men from childhood...and all men enjoy works of imitation."[1] Thus, our response to beauty and art is natural (not derived from some other aspect of human nature), and the essence of beauty and art is that they delight. While Aristotle's equation of art with imitation may not seem to square with much of modern art, I think that it is generally correct. Art is a kind of making or creating, and while the artist (say a painter or musician) may not be trying to imitate a particular thing, it remains that the action of creating is imitating the coming into being of things which we experience on many levels. However, whatever one wants to say about the fine arts, it is clear that such forms of literature as depict human beings in action (drama, epics, novels, etc.) are acts of imitation–not perhaps of any actual person acting, but of human action.

Aristotle defines tragedy as

> an imitation of an action which is serious and complete and has a proper magnitude, rendered with speech made pleasing separately in the parts of each of its different divisions, presented dramatically and not by means of narrative, and ending in, by means of pity and fear, catharsis of such emotions.[2]

The parts Aristotle has in mind are: plot, character, thought, language, sung lyrics, and spectacle.[3] Comedy would seem to have all the same parts as tragedy but lacks its serious theme and the catharsis by means of pity and fear.[4] Aristotle says that epic has the same parts as tragedy (including the reversals, recognitions, and sufferings that bring about pity and fear), excepting song and spectacle.[5]

Given this general definition of what literature is, the question can be raised: what makes a good play or epic? A good piece of literature ought to evoke wonder and delight.[6] If it does not do this, then it has failed, even if it has given accurate historical, physical, or ethical information. While issues of truth and morality do occur in stories, they are not of central concern. Consider this key text:

> Correctness for the poetic art is not the same as for politics or any other art. Within the poetic art itself mistakes are of two kinds: (a) essential and (b) accidental....If the poet describes an impossible object in relation to the art itself, he makes a mistake. But the description is correct, provided that the end of the poetic art is attained; for the end is enhanced, if in this way that description makes the corresponding part or some other part of the poem more striking.[7]

The essential purpose of art is not to provide information, whether historical,[8] or physical/metaphysical,[9] or ethical.[10]

Plot is the most important element, since it is upon the quality of the plot that the success of the work of literature depends.[11] A good plot is one which has a clear beginning, middle, and end and which is unified around one action which is as complex and of as great a magnitude as its unity allows. Key to a good plot are reversals and recognitions since these are surprising and hence the source of wonder and delight. The best plot is one in which these reversals and recognitions come about by necessity, that is, by the necessity set up by the story. The other parts–character, thought, language, sung lyrics, and spectacle–also contribute to the quality of the play and are listed in order of importance.[12] However, none of these can replace deficiency in plot; character and thought are successful not by themselves, but insofar as they support the plot. For example, while Aristotle says that the main character in both tragedy and epic should be as good or better than we are, this is not in order to teach us morality, but so that the work may have its proper effect of arousing pity and fear and in general wonder and delight. So also, the reasonableness of the thought process is important in making the plot plausible and so powerful, not for the sake of teaching us logic or correct reasoning about the things of this world.[13]

Given the danger in a Great Books Seminar of distorting a discipline by seeing it though the eyes of another discipline or by attempting to find some transcendent method to create an interdisciplinary understanding, it might seem that the Great Books Seminar is bound for trouble. It is true that it is difficult to sort out the essential features of a text from those which happen to be in the text but are there to serve those essential features, but this is actually the strength of the "great books" or "core text" method: it challenges the student to consider the many different realms of intelligibility open to the human mind. In an age where the scientific/technological paradigm with its demands for specialization tends to dominate, there is the grave danger of adopting one set of principles or one viewpoint for everything. To understand that the essence of ethics cannot be reached by scientific method, that great literature is not reducible to ethical themes, that history is not reducible to metaphysics, nor metaphysics to historical conditions, is to guard against the enslavement of the human spirit. To understand the proper limits of disciplines is to prevent the hegemony of any one method which, since it obviously cannot handle all the aspects of our intellectual experience, may lead to mental confusion and frustration, and perhaps to the loss of trust in human reason. In the Great Books Seminar, the student must move between disciplines often, sometimes with every work studied. Here is a great opportunity to keep the various dimensions of human knowing awake, constantly renewing the intellectual life of the student.

Notes

1. Aristotle, *Poetics*, 4 (1488b5-9) in *Aristotle Selected Works*, tr. Hippocrates G. Apostle and Lloyd P. Gerson (Grinnell, Iowa: The Peripatetic

Press, 1982).

2. Ibid., 6 (1449b24-28).

3. Ibid., 6 (1550a8-10).

4. Comedies such as those of Shakespeare do in fact involve serious themes in parts, as well as tensions of fear and pity; these tensions are, however, resolved in the end in a happy way.

5. Ibid., 24 (1459b8-14).

6. Ibid., 4 (1488b5-19); 24 (1460a12-18).

7. Ibid., 25 (1460b15-27).

8. As Aristotle says when discussing the epic, "its compositions should not be like those histories which must present not a single action but all the chance and unrelated happenings to one or more persons during a single period" (ibid., 23 [1459a22-25]).

9. "With respect to the making of poetry, a convincing impossibility is preferable to an unconvincing possibility" (ibid., 25 [1461b12-3]).

10. "As to whether something was nobly or ignobly said or done, one should examine the problem by attending not only to whether the thing done or said was good or bad, but also to the man who performed the deed or spoke" (ibid., 25 [1461a5-8]); that is, the action should fit the character.

11. It is interesting to note that even within the parts of tragedy (and literature in general) there is one part which is essential: "the plot, then, is the principle and, as it were, the soul of tragedy" (ibid., [1450a39]). Each of the other parts belongs essentially to another field and is used by the artist in the service of literature's proper end. Thus, character is essentially a matter for ethics, thought for logic/rhetoric/dialectic, language for grammar, sung lyrics for music, and spectacle for the visual arts.

12. Aristotle goes so far as to say that the greatness of a tragedy comes across when it is read as well as performed. This is not to say that the other parts are unimportant, just that they must serve the plot. In fact, one of the reasons why Aristotle thinks that tragedy is superior to epic is that it involves sung lyrics and spectacle. While least important to the tragedy, they are a source of delight and hence a part of what is artistic about the play. It is just that if any of these lesser parts claims its own due, apart from its relation to the plot, then the play as a whole is weakened.

13. Aristotle does say that it is "right to censure a poet for using what is unreasonable or evil without any necessity" (ibid., 25 [1461b19-20]). However, this does not mean that quality of thought and character are in themselves tests of the greatness of a tragedy. What is meant is that, if not necessitated by the plot, then bad reasoning or immorality provides suitable grounds for criticising a play. If, on the other hand, it serves the plot, then the poor reasoning or immoral action is not suitable grounds for criticism.

Beginnings and Endings Among the Two Chief World Systems

Anne Leavitt

Malaspina University-College

Every two years, I am introduced to a new group of third-year students with whom, for the next four semesters, I will journey through a great number of great works in the Western tradition. My role is that of tour guide and occasional interpreter although, as time goes on, the students are increasingly expected to take on these roles for themselves and each other.

But the Liberal Studies Program at Malaspina University-College on Vancouver Island (off the southwest coast of British Columbia) tries to do more than offer students seminar opportunities for discussing many of the great books and works of music and art in the Western tradition. Intermittently, during their time in the Program, students are asked to participate in five- or six-week science modules designed not so much to instruct them as to immerse them in the intellectual experience that undergirds the history of science in the West.

A number of my colleagues outside the Liberal Studies Program are understandably skeptical about these modules—especially our astronomy module. It has become almost a commonplace among some members of the Faculty of Humanities that having non-science students puzzle over original scientific texts is nothing less than cruel and unusual punishment. When I point out that the texts are reasonably accessible to anyone with the somewhat reflective smattering of Euclidean geometry which our students acquire before they approach astronomy, their skepticism hardly diminishes. "Original texts?" goes the exclamation, "Surely you can't be serious! What original astronomical works have been written in the past few years that presume only a smattering of Euclidean geometry?" None at all of course. That's why we don't ask our students to read recent works in astronomy. Rather, they are asked to consider short selections from Aristotle, Ptolemy, and Aristarchus, and end with a romp through Galileo's *Dialogue Concerning the Two Chief World Systems*. My skeptical colleagues are right, of course, when they point out that all of the astronomy in these works is terribly out of date but their question, "So what's the point?" can, in fact, be answered.

Let me answer it by telling you what we do. And, as I describe to you what it is we do, I'd like you to consider something T. S. Eliot says in "Little Gidding," the fourth of his *Four Quartets*:

> What we call the beginning is often the end
> And to make an end is to make a beginning.
> The end is where we start from.

(216-9)

One of the first things we ask of our students is that they look at the stars. Now, this is a difficult thing for most students to do no matter who they are. Most have never taken a particularly long look at what's up there and confess that they have no real idea what they should be looking at when they do. To make matters worse, our astronomy module falls during the rainy season on the West Coast. Between early November and late March, our island is enveloped in a thick blanket of cloud.

One way to address this problem is to allow students access to a planetarium and this, in effect, is what we do. Each purchases an inexpensive shareware program (*Skyglobe*) which presents them a picture of the night sky at a position, date and time that they choose.[1] They can view the sky from any direction and watch celestial phenomena move in real time or over months, years and even millennia. In class, we use the program to look at the sky from a number of geographical locations at different times of the year. We also look at the strange, regularly irregular behavior of the lights we know as planets and the particularly erratic monthly and yearly behavior of the light we know as the moon. And we ask students to begin to think about whether there might be useful explanatory models for the behavior of these bodies–models that might account for such things as surprise them like the midnight sun at the North Pole in summer and the fact that the inner planets never stray too far from the sun in their risings and settings.

It is here that they run into their greatest and most interesting problem with the study of astronomy and it turns out that this problem has important ramifications for more than their approach to celestial phenomena. The problem is not so much that they have spent little time looking at the stars. The problem is the position from which they begin to look at the stars. In the beginning of our inquiry, they are all heliocentrists–they are deeply and absolutely convinced that the earth and other planets travel around the sun. And yet, no matter how valiant their attempts, most of them cannot at all see how the celestial phenomena they have been contemplating can be at all accounted for by the model they've believed in since kindergarten.

This is very interesting, don't you think? Imagine a group of reasonably capable students who are absolutely convinced that the earth and the planets travel around the sun and who also believe that to think otherwise is tantamount to lunacy. They believe in a heliocentric view of the solar system as firmly as they believe in anything, and they believe that they believe this theory because they believe they know that it is true. They are then offered years and years of direct observations of the movements of the celestial bodies, none of which could possibly constitute evidence that the earth and planets travel around the sun. This, of course, does not trouble them, at least not initially. They valiantly work away at using the heliocentric model to account for what they have observed, though not usually for very long. The task is too much but they are sure that it has been done and can be done, if not by them then by somebody else. We ask them how they know this. It takes a bit of time, but in the end all admit that they know this because this is what they've always been told. We ask what evidence they have that might suggest that what they've been told is right. "None at all."

It is at this moment that we are ready to begin our study of some of the core texts of the Western astronomical tradition. But we do not begin where they would be most at ease. At this point, they are keen to begin the study of Galileo's *Dialogue Concerning the Two Chief World Systems* which, they happily expect, will return them to the heliocentric solar system they desperately want to believe they inhabit. Where they began, with a heliocentric model of the solar system, will indeed be where we end. But not before they have made for themselves a beginning in the world which Galileo helped bring to an end.

We do this by having them read and discuss selections from Aristotle's *On the Heavens* and Ptolemy's *Almagest*. The results are interesting. The elegance and explanatory power of the models of nested celestial spheres and of the planets pursuing the path of the sun in coiling epicycles immediately capture their imaginations and they find themselves terribly impressed with the predictive capacities of the Ptolemeic system.

They are also asked to consider some of the work of Aristarchus of Samos (fl. 270 BCE), the "Copernicus" of the ancient world. And while they rightly appreciate his demonstrations of the relative distances of the sun and moon from the earth, the length of the moon's diameter relative to the earth and the relative sizes of the sun and moon, they quickly come to see why his heliocentric theory was not widely accepted. Aristarchus could not explain two important things (and neither can they): why it is that things don't fly off the earth if the earth is really spinning, and why the effects of parallax are not observable for the stars if the earth is really moving around the sun. By the time they begin Galileo, these are questions they need him to answer before they'll allow him to return them to the heliocentric solar system they want to believe they live in. They now understand that theological prejudice alone could not have been responsible for the great, centuries-long hold of the geocentric model on the understanding of educated Europeans. They too want a reasoned defense of what even they have begun to see is a highly questionable proposition–that the earth and planets travel around the sun.

Few of our students have great difficulties navigating their way through Galileo's *Dialogue Concerning the Two Chief World Systems.* It is written, after all, as a conversation among three figures–a Copernican (Salviati), a scholastic (Simplicio), and a man (Sagredo), not unlike our students, who is torn between the two chief models of the heavens. The conversation is quite readable and students find themselves wondering at the degree to which the success of Galileo's model rested as much upon the satire of the poor Simplicio (with whom some identify, somewhat to their discomfort) as upon anything else. They are surprised to discover the extent to which the power of Galileo's presentation is due to rhetorical effects which they consider out of place in scientific inquiry. This, in itself, makes for a useful discussion.

But much of their astonishment is raised by the beginning of the text which, initially, baffles them. Reading Galileo for the first time, most students expect him to begin with an all-out, frontal assault upon the geocentric model of the solar-system. Instead, they find a long, detailed discussion of the motions of inanimate objects up and down, along inclined planes and around in circles. They recall that Aristotle talked about motion, and that he insisted that the heavens move uniformly and circularly; but most found the details of Aristotle's discussion uninteresting. They are surprised to find that the most ordinary of things–the motion of an inanimate object–can be the subject of such controversy and analysis. They become persuaded by Galileo's conclusion, that motion in a straight line is either accelerating or decelerating motion and that the only uniform motion is circular motion. But it is not until they work through his discussion on projectiles–the arcing movement made by such things as spit-balls–that they appreciate Galileo's genius in finding the earth-shattering in the ordinary. For it is the same arcing movement of the spit-ball, when analyzed in light of the laws of circular and linear motion, which supplies the explanation of how it is that things on the earth are not tossed into space by the earth's circular motion. This explanation, when put together with Galileo's lucid analysis of how Copernicus' model can account for such observed phenomena as the retrograde motion of the planets, provides the heliocentric model with the support it needs to be considered a serious rival of the geocentric model.

What my students don't find is the proof they're looking for that the heliocentric model is the only model. They accept Galileo's conclusion, drawn from his peeks through the telescope, that the stars are too far away for the effects of parallax to be observed. And they accept his conclusion that the presence of mountains on the moon suggests that the earth and other planets are not as different as they might seem. His observations of the moons of Jupiter suggest to him and to them that the earth can't be the only center of all motion in the heavens just as his observations of the behavior of sun-spots suggests that even the sun spins on its axis. They find the conclusions Galileo draws from these seemingly insignificant things to be brilliant just as they find the conclusions he draws from the apparently insignificant motions of projectiles to be brilliant. All agree, however, that Galileo does not give them the they proof they would like.

What's interesting is their response to his overall approach. Galileo shows so many of the Aristotelian appeals to formal and final causes to be not only highly speculative but ridiculous that my students become persuaded that the geometrical description of physical phenomena which leads to certainty is the best approach to astronomical and physical matters.[2] And they become persuaded that Galileo's hypothesis that earthly and heavenly phenomena fall under the same natural laws is more fruitful for understanding the heavens than the older Aristotelian hypothesis that the laws which governed them must be different. They also understand that Ptolemy is somewhat immune to most of the criticisms Galileo lays at Aristotle's door. Above all, it is the elegance and simplicity of the heliocentric model that appeals to them. Galileo may not give them the proof they would like, but he gives them confidence to believe that their belief in a heliocentric solar system is, at least, rational.

All of this is not to say that Galileo leads them cheerfully out of the ancient world into the modern. As much as the power of Galileo's method seems to them to hold great promise, they worry about the implications of its extension to explain the movements of human beings. They wonder if all discussion of formal and final causes should really have no place in any scientific inquiry and they wonder whether Galileo's own work does not suggest that imaginative speculation has more to do with scientific understanding than they might have expected.[3] In studying Galileo, they end with their beginning and, in this ending, are several more beginnings.

In the same poem I quoted earlier, T. S. Eliot offers what could easily be the motto for our astronomy module in the Liberal Studies Program at Malaspina. He says:

> We shall not cease from exploration
> And the end of our exploring
> Will be to arrive where we started
> And know the place for the first time.

(241-4)

To the extent that one follows such a motto, the teaching of science through core texts can offer undergraduates a wealth of new beginnings among ideas which, in the beginning, they believe they already understand.

Works Cited

Eliot. T. S. *Four Quartets.* New York: Harcourt, Brace and Company, 1943.

Einstein, Albert. Preface. *Dialogue Concerning the Two Chief World Systems–Ptolemeic and Copernican.* Trans. Stillman Drake. 2nd ed. Berkeley: University of California, 1967.

Galilei, Galileo. *Dialogue Concerning the Two Chief World Systems–Ptolemeic and Copernican.* Trans. Stillman Drake. 2nd ed. Berkeley: University of California, 1967.

Notes

1. *Skyglobe* (Copyright, Mark A. Haney, 1993) is distributed by KlassM Software, Ann Arbor, Michigan.

2. Galileo's explanation and defense of this approach can be found on pages 101-4 of Stillman Drake's translation of the *Dialogue Concerning the Two Chief World Systems*

3. In his preface to Stillman Drake's translation of the *Dialogue Concerning the Two Chief World Systems*, Albert Einstein makes the following observation:

> It has often been maintained that Galileo became the father of modern science by replacing the speculative, deductive method with the empirical, experimental method...[However], there is no empirical method without speculative concepts and systems; and there is no speculative thinking whose concepts do not reveal... the empirical method from which they stem. To put into sharp contrast the empirical and the deductive attitude is misleading, and was utterly foreign to Galileo. (xvii)

Assessing Scientific Claims:

Darwin and Creationism

Thomas L. Wymer

Bowling Green University

One of our major concerns as educators, especially in core courses, is teaching critical thinking. At the same time, in our pluralistic and multicultural society we are supposed to respect diversity of opinion. These two concerns inevitably intersect at times, and nowhere is there more potential for explosive intersection than in discussions of evolution. My concern, however, is that these explosions, at least these intersections, happen too infrequently. There are lots of reasons why this is so, the worst of which–and this is the major problem in secondary science education–is that instructors are afraid of the controversy likely to result outside the classroom in contexts like school boards. In such classrooms, students are either directly misinformed or left uninformed. And even where such outside controversy is not a concern, biology instructors have enough to do to explain the current paradigm and don't feel they have the time to justify it, especially because within the legitimate scientific community the evolutionary model is unquestioned. Certainly there are continuing debates about specific mechanisms that drive evolution, but there is simply no serious alternative scientific model. Nevertheless, confusion and misinformation persist and, within the context of colleges and universities, emerge especially in general studies courses like one I teach called Great Ideas.

Great Ideas is an interdisciplinary lower division course that seeks to form the basis for an understanding in students of some of the major issues and movements that make up the intellectual heritage of Western culture. We explore such bodies of ideas as the Judeo-Christian-Islamic tradition, philosophy and rationalism, the scientific revolution, democracy, economics and class, and multiculturalism. The science chapter focuses on two major revolutions in scientific thought, the Copernican and the Darwinian, and seeks to provide the basis for intelligent assessment of scientific controversies. Generally students have little difficulty with the Copernican revolution since they see the issues raised there as settled and nonthreatening, but they have difficulty applying the lessons they might learn from the earlier revolution to the later one, and instructors often have difficulty resolving the resulting disputes.

How students may respond to this issue is likely to vary somewhat from class to class in any particular college, and from one part of the country to another. At a state university like Bowling Green there is never a class full of creationists, but there always seems to be a small but vocal group of them, while the majority of the class, though having no special objection to evolutionary theory, seem ill-equipped to deal with the popular controversies surrounding it. I would like to offer here not a pedagogical approach, but an analysis of the problem that may open the way to any number of pedagogical solutions, including choice of core texts.

In my classes there are two major misunderstandings that repeatedly arise. The first is the tendency of many students to refer to creation science as "the Christian theory." They do so in spite of the fact that most of the major theological seminaries in the nation, Christian and Jewish alike, accept evolution as a viable theory and do not see creationism as any kind of *scientific* alternative. Among Roman Catholics, in fact, the issue was clarified recently when Pope John Paul II announced just last October the view of the Church that "fresh knowledge leads to recognition of the theory of evolution as more than just a hypothesis."[1] The essential matter of doctrine that the Church insists on, this announcement says, is this: "If the human body has its origin in living material which preexists it, the spiritual soul is immediately created by God." That, of course, is an issue about which science cannot speak with any authority.

This distinction between the things of the spirit, about which religion can speak, and the things of the material world, about which science can speak, satisfies most theologians and would satisfy the concerns of science education if the body of fundamentalist believers, including a few academically credentialed ones who continue to call themselves creation scientists, did not do such an effective job of confusing the issues. This leads to the second major kind of misunderstanding that emerges in my classes, the belief expressed by many students that the opposing claims of evolutionists and creationists are unresolvable and equally plausible matters of faith. In other words, many of them continue to swallow the creationist equal-time argument in spite of federal court having confirmed in 1982 that laws sanctioning the introduction of creationism into the science classroom under the guise of "balanced treatment" were unconstitutional attempts to advance particular religious beliefs.[2]

Certainly the question of whether or not there is a god who is ultimately responsible for the existence of the material world is a legitimate question that can be answered only by faith, but the claim that divine acts of creation are in any way observable or demonstrable by scientific means is totally without foundation. So why does the belief persist that there is any scientific plausibility in creationist claims?

The answer is closely related to the question of why scientists get so upset about this issue. In fact, an enormous amount of scientific writing directed toward the general public has appeared in the last decade or two, and a considerable portion of that has been driven by the creationist controversy. Biologists, of course, are concerned that students be properly introduced to the current dominant paradigm in their discipline, and they are disturbed that the efforts of creationists have shaped widely used textbooks and dictated the way biology is taught in innumerable schools across the country, but it goes deeper than that. It goes to the very foundations of science itself.

The problem begins with the fact that the typical response of religion to science is to insist that science does not have all the answers in order to maintain a space for religious faith. This is what I like to call the argument from ignorance.

The argument from ignorance can certainly be a reasonable approach–after all, science doesn't have all the answers. The question of whether we possess immortal souls is a case in point. This kind of argument becomes much more problematical, however, when it is applied to material things. If I don't know why the sun rises and sets or why it rains, I can always posit God as the answer. The weakness here is that I have to keep shifting my ground as more and more such issues are adequately explained as natural phenomena. This is why the most reasonable theologians accept current estimates of the age of the universe and see creation as an extended process beginning with something like the Big Bang. The argument from ignorance works at that point since by definition there can be no conceivable record of anything that happened before such a singularity. But most creationists claim greater ignorance, and the special advantage for them is that as knowledge advances, those explanations become more and more complicated and more difficult to understand; it therefore becomes easier to claim ignorance about matters that are in fact pretty well understood.

It is not likely to strike anyone as a profound insight that the two misunderstandings I have noted are based on ignorance. But it is important for us to recognize the extent to which the spokesmen for so-called scientific creationism foster this kind of ignorance.

One example relates to a problem that Darwin himself recognized, the incompleteness of the fossil record and the lack of sufficient examples of "intermediate forms" to create a complete history of evolutionary developments. The fact is that a great many such intermediate forms have since been discovered, providing many so-called missing links as well as reasonably detailed histories of several phyla. But creationists either ignore this evidence or cite Darwin's own acknowledgment that "the geological record...does not yield the infinitely many fine gradations between past and present species required on the theory." It is still true in the study of *macro*biota that however detailed a fossil record may have accumulated, in any particular dig, as a paleontologist has told me, they are lucky if they find a well-preserved dinosaur fossil, for example, every fifty meters. The fossil record still falls far short of those infinite gradations. But over the last several decades paleontologists looking at the fossils of *micro*biota in sedimentary rocks laid down over billions of years can find in a single core sample evidence of thousands of developing microspecies *every millimeter,* revealing a highly detailed history of development fully consistent with evolutionary theory and quite literally bordering on the infinitely fine gradations Darwin dreamed of. Such stratographic research, combined with increasingly sophisticated radiometric data, has produced in addition much more accurate dating of biological eras as far back as the Precambrian. Creationists, however, prefer to focus on macrolife, where they can find solace in the greater gaps in our knowledge. Indeed, creationists like to deal with evolutionary theory in terms of Darwin in part so that they can claim a nineteenth-century degree of ignorance in the theory.

These examples reveal some of the problems inherent in using a core text like *Origin of Species.* Although Darwin's central premise survives, there are significant differences between the specifics of "Darwinism" as Darwin was able to argue it in the middle of the nineteenth century and "Darwinism" as the word may be used to describe evolutionary theory today. This should not surprise us since Darwin knew nothing about genetics, much less DNA or genetic engineering. However great his contribution, Darwin had his limitations, which any honest analysis must acknowledge, but without some understanding of the state of evolutionary theory today as well as in Darwin's time, we cannot assess those limitations properly. I have already discussed the incompleteness of the fossil record, but there is another issue that Darwin was even less able to deal with, the problem of the varying rates of evolutionary development revealed by the fossil record.

A major division of thought among geologists in Darwin's time was that between uniformitarians and gradualists on the one hand, and catastrophists on the other. The former associated themselves with what continues to be a fundamental premise of geology and biology today and was expressed in the title of a book Darwin knew, Charles Lyell's *Principles of Geology, Being an Attempt to Explain the Former Changes of the Earth's Surface, by Reference to Causes Now in Operation*; in addition they believed that the operation of these laws brought about changes that took place slowly by the gradual accumulation of small changes over long periods of time. Catastrophism, on the other hand, was associated with attempts to describe geological change in terms of divine intervention like Noah's Flood. Catastrophists seemed to be supported, however, by features in the fossil record that came to be described as mass extinctions and subsequent "explosions" of new forms of life. These in fact define geologic eras. The best known of these is the Cretaceous-Tertiary boundary, when dinosaurs went extinct, but the most dramatic in terms of the percentage of species lost and replaced is the Precambrian-Cambrian boundary. Darwin's model of natural selection based on random variation did not seem to provide an adequate explanation for these kinds of change. Moreover, because of the religious associations of catastrophism, this issue was not adequately faced up to by Darwin or, until quite recently, by the scientific community—not until 1972 when Stephen Jay Gould and Niles Eldredge published their punctuated equilibrium theory.

Whether we want to see this as evidence of dishonesty in science or as an inevitable part of the process of development of any theory, the presence of gaps which, it was believed, further research would fill in, in this case the theory was vindicated. The very next year after the Gould and Eldredge announcement Stanley H. Cohen and Herbert W. Boyer showed that DNA can be cut and rejoined with specific enzymes, a discovery that soon led to the realization that bacteria "invented" the process of recombining DNA as much as three and a half billion years ago and that evolutionary change could in fact proceed by a process of natural selection much more rapidly than supposed, especially in times like those following mass extinctions when all sorts of ecological niches would be vacant. Moreover, the Alvarez impact theory, announced in 1980, has stimulated all sorts of research into these boundary areas, which has greatly expanded our knowledge not only of such impacts, but of other triggers of mass extinctions like periods of vulcanism, of sea-level variation, of high or low concentrations of greenhouse gases, and of ice ages. As a result, these processes can be explained now in considerable detail without recourse to divine intervention, not even to the invisible hand of some kind of "intelligent design," the latest gimmick of creationists to introduce religion into the science classroom.

Finally, in the context of this discussion that attempt makes clear that the central argument behind creationism, the argument from design, is itself a variant of the argument from ignorance. The argument is in fact based, as Daniel C. Dennett points out, simply on the inability to "imagine how anything other than an Intelligent Artificer could be the cause of the adaptations that anyone could observe."[3]

But, as Dennett and many others argue, scientists know a great deal more now not only about what happened, but about how these adaptations could happen, how in more general terms complex adaptive systems emerge every day out of simple conditions in thermodynamically open contexts. Complexity theory is yet another major area of investigation that has emerged in the last thirty or forty years and which creationists, in order to maintain their position, must ignore or dismiss. This is why so many of their arguments are attacks on science itself. In order to maintain their argument from ignorance, many of them, not content with the actual limitations on knowledge that we all suffer from, attempt not simply to expose ignorance, but to create it, to claim ignorance in contexts where we know a great deal. They seek to confuse issues about what science does, how it asks questions, tests hypotheses, assesses evidence, draws conclusions, builds on past knowledge–in short, the whole endeavor–so that a space can be created for asserting *as scientific theory* what is in fact a theological position based not on any disciplined observation of nature but on a three thousand-year-old text. In order to claim that their position is scientific, in other words, they must create radical confusion not only about what science knows, but about what it is. Their attack, therefore, is not simply on the theory of evolution; it is on science itself. It is especially ironic and a source of additional confusion that they then attempt to clothe their counterclaims in the mantle of science and not at all surprising that legitimate scientists would be angered and frustrated by such attacks.

It should be clear, therefore, that any attempt to explore evolutionary theory using Darwin as a core text needs to be considerably supplemented by more recent studies, if any real understanding of the theory is expected. To that end, a list of readable books on this topic is appended to this discussion.

Notes

1. Reported in *New York Times,* 25 October 1996. This does not even represent a major change in the Church's position, but, as the *Times* explains, it does take a step beyond an encyclical letter from Pope Pius XII in 1950, which ac-

cepted Darwin's views as "a serious hypothesis" but cautioned that while not in itself objectionable that hypothesis played into the hands of materialists and atheists.
2. See Marcel C. La Follette, ed., *Creationism, Science, and the Law* (Cambridge: MIT Press, 1983).
3. *Darwin's Dangerous Idea: Evolution and the Meaning of Life* (New York: Simon & Schuster, 1995), 47.

Science and Scientific Controversy: A Select Bibliography

General
Brockman, John. *The Third Culture: Beyond the Scientific Revolution.* New York: Simon & Schuster, 1995.
Bronowski, Jacob. *Science and Human Values.* rev. ed. New York: Harper & Row, 1965.
Cohen, J. Berhard. *Revolution in Science.* Cambridge: Harvard University Press, 1985.
Engelhardt, H. Tristram and Arthur L. Caplan, eds. *Scientific Controversies: Case Studies in the Resolution and Closure of Disputes in Science and Technology.* Cambridge: Cambridge University Press, 1987.
Friedlander, Michael W. *At the Fringes of Science.* Boulder: Westview, 1995.
Johnson, George. *Fire in the Mind: Science, Faith, and the Search for Order.* New York: Knopf, 1996.
Sagan, Carl. *The Demon-Haunted World: Science as a Candle in the Dark.* New York: Random House, 1996.

Bioscience
Aldridge, Susan. *The Thread of Life: The Story of Genes and Genetic Engineering.* Cambridge: Cambridge University Press, 1996.
Angier, Natalie. *The Beauty of the Beastly: New Views of the Nature of life.* Boston: Houghton Mifflin, 1995.
Cziko, Gary. *Without Miracles: Universal Selection Theory and the Second Darwinian Revolution.* Cambridge: MIT Press, 1996.
Dawkins, Richard. The Blind Watchmaker: Why the Evidence of Evolution Reveals a Universe without Design. New York: Norton, 1986
———. *River Out of Eden:* A Danvinian View of Life. New York: Basic, 1995
———. *Climbing Mount Improbable.* New York· Norton, 1996.
de Duve, Christian. *Vital Dust: Life as a Cosmic Imperative.* New York: Basic, 1995.
Dennett, Daniel C. *Darwin's Dangerous Idea: Evolution and the Meanings of Life.* New York: Simon & Schuster, 1995.
Margulis, Lynn and Dorian Sagan. *Microcosmos: Four Billion Years of Evolution from Our Microbial Ancestors.* New York: Summit, 1986.
Tudge, Colin. *The Engineer in the Garden, Genes and Genetics: From the Idea of Heredity to the Creation of Life.* New York: Hill & Wang, 1995 (originally published London, 1993).

Complexity and Chaos

Casti, John L. *Would-Be Worlds: How the New Science of Simulation Is Breaking the Complexity Barrier*. New York: Wiley, 1997.

Cohen, Jack and Ian Stewart. *The Collapse of Chaos: Discovering Simplicity in a Complex World*. New York: Viking, 1994.

Coveney, Peter and Roger Highfield. *Frontiers of Complexity: The Search for Order in a Chaotic World*. New York: Fawcett-Ballantine, 1995.

Holland, John H. *Hidden Order: How Adaptation Builds Complexity*. Reading, MA: Addison-Wesley, 1995.

Kauffman, Stuart. *At Home in the Universe: The Search for the Laws of Self-Organization and Complexity*. Oxford University Press, 1995.

Lewin, Roger. *Complexity: Life at the Edge of Chaos*. New York: Macmillan, 1992.

Seeing What Is Not One's Own:

Herodotus, Ethnography, and the Concept of Shame

Kathleen A. Hull

New York University

What I would like to do today is to talk about reading Herodotus' *Histories*, and to invite you into a class of thoughtful eighteen-year-olds who had some interesting and, I think, rather profound responses to one of Herodotus' cultural observations while visiting Egypt. In short, I would like to show you one example of how this text can work in a classroom. In addition, I will suggest here that Herodotus' method of doing history displays and repeats itself in the classroom, as we seek to interpret his interpretations.

Yesterday at one of our plenary sessions, Steve Zelnick mentioned how important it is for teachers to excite students' imaginations. Herodotus manages to excite without any help from academics. The thematic use of his *Histories* in the recent Academy Award-winning film *The English Patient* shows us that even Hollywood recognizes the imaginative power of Herodotus!

The framework for my discussion here comes from Seth Benardete's *Herodotean Inquiries*.[1] As every beginning student of Herodotus learns, Herodotus believes that eyes are more trustworthy than ears for gathering data, or, as the scholars say, autopsy–"being there"–is more reliable than hearsay. The importance of seeing for oneself is established

early on in the *Histories*. We begin with the familiar story of the origins
of the destruction of the Lydian kingship in Book I. Candaules wants
his favorite bodyguard, Gyges, to *see* his wife naked so that Gyges will
believe that Candaules' wife is the most beautiful of all women. For
Candaules, hearsay is not adequate to establish belief. How can Gyges
really believe that she is the most beautiful woman only on the basis of
Candaules' prejudiced report? Gyges initially refuses Candaules' offer,
and responds that "every man should look [only] to his own" (1.7). To
see things that are "not one's own" is to break a Lydian taboo about
shame, namely, that we should not openly look at others when they are
"in shame," that is to say, in actions, situations, or compromising positions considered shameful by the community. In the story, of course,
Candaules eventually succeeds at getting Gyges to see what is not his
own (namely, Candaules' naked wife), and thus gets Gyges to break a
taboo. The fallout from this transgression includes not only the end of
the naïve happiness of these three individuals, but also the beginnings
of eventual war and the end of an empire.

The theme I want to develop is that "seeing what is not one's own" is
always taboo. Further, I would suggest that whenever we try to see and
believe and understand another culture or community–that which is not
our own–we are breaking this universal taboo. Herodotus recognizes
these taboos. However, according to Herodotean historiography, nothing is *truly* taboo, in the sense that Herodotus is continually willing to
break this taboo against the otherness of the other in his practice as a
historian. Similarly, he invites his Greek readers to break every taboo
against seeing "the other," the *barbaros*, by reading his book. And so,
in the same way that Candaules got Gyges to see what was not his own,
so Herodotus gets the Greek reader to see things that are not his own,
namely, non-Greek culture.

Usually, we call this Herodotus' "enthusiasm for a foreign culture,"
but we might just as easily call it his enthusiasm for the shameful. He's
not afraid to examine and explore what *seems* shameful to himself.
However, his own "flinchings"–reactions to what seems shameful–are
not automatic signs to him that his own culture has the correct standards and others are obviously wrong; rather, his flinching serves as a
sign that *here* is where the power of *nomos* in the culture needs to be
further explored. The *Histories* are an inquiry and an investigation in
the deepest sense–for Herodotus explores otherness by paying attention
to the self's response to it.

Now, Herodotus knows full well that what is considered shameful can
only be understood within the context of a community–that is, in relation to a particular community's mores and laws. When he gets to
Egypt, in Book II, he notes that everything there was upside down in
comparison to Greek customs (2.36). For example, in Egypt people

defecate indoors and eat out of doors, he reports; and this is the opposite of the Greeks. The logic behind this, he says, is "that one must perform shameful necessities secretly and those that are not shameful
openly" (2.36). What attracts Herodotus is just what differs from what
is known in Greece.

This brings us to the discussion in my class last semester. In a passage about the extreme reverence shown to sacred animals by the
Egyptians, Herodotus mentions that in one district in Egypt, all goats
are revered, all goatherds are esteemed, and that the entire district goes
into mourning when one of its goats dies (2.46). He then writes,
"Something monstrous happened in my presence in this district...a
woman openly had sex with a billy goat. It showed me something about
humanity" (2.46). The event is a prime example of Herodotus at work.
Because he has referred to it as "monstrous," we can see that it has,
indeed, evoked a large reaction–a flinching, if you will–from him. And
yet, we see how much he strives for objectivity. He does not presume to
know the woman's motive, nor does he explain to the reader what he
learned about human nature at that moment. As usual, he tends not to
draw the moral, but to leave the inference to the reader.[2] Here we find
ourselves deep within the basic problem of all historiography: what is
the relationship between the so-called facts and the interpretation of
what it means, for us? Herodotus is not unaware of the difficulties of
trying to transfer a truthful account of an observation to another person.[3]

When I asked my students what *they* thought Herodotus had learned
about human nature as a result of witnessing the woman and the goat,
there were three responses. The first student said that he thought it was
significant that the sex was performed *openly*. This was a good observation since, as we've seen, Herodotus says that in Egypt what is done
openly is clean and not shameful, while what is done secretly is unclean
and shameful. The second student suggested that Herodotus learned
that human nature and animal nature are quite close–a possible interpretation, though problematic, given other things that he says about
Egyptian religion and morals. However, the third student's response
was the most surprising, to me. She suggested that what Herodotus
learned by seeing a woman openly having sex with a goat was how
spiritual or *religious* human beings are. Referring to the earlier passages on the sacredness of goats, the student said that the woman may
have been trying to unite with a sacred object or symbol, perhaps ritu-
ally. From the viewpoint of current scholarship, this was a fine interpretation.[4]

As these thoughtful students pondered Herodotus' ambivalent report,
another level of question emerged. What establishes a sense of shame
for us? Is it natural? Where does it come from? How do I judge

whether to respect or despise myself? We discussed these questions. Herodotus teaches us that the concept of shame assumes a community whose public values define what is shameful, and that any particular community has its own views of what is shameful or not. In contrast, in today's American culture, old senses of shame seem to be largely disappearing, as individuals more and more seek personal fulfillment outside of community contexts, and as religious communities have so profoundly lost their power to influence individual conscience.

But let's go back to that woman and goat. What of Herodotus' strong adjective for the bestiality he observed? He says it was "monstrous"! This remark is somewhat surprising from the historian/observer whom many scholars have praised for offering the clinical stance of a dispassionate researcher and who has come to be viewed as a cultural and moral relativist!

Although on moral questions Herodotus tends to maintain a quite remarkable objectivity, his openness to alien cultures is not without bounds. Herodotus may still be seen as trying "to discover the human beneath the infinite disguises of custom."[5] There is little doubt that Herodotus gave up the conviction that only his own (Greek) customs were valid, and that those of everyone else were wrong. However, a moot question remains: is Herodotus still inquiring about whether any judgments about the customs and laws of those from other cultures can be made? Is human nature so completely culturally determined, that no judgments about the "inhumanity" of other cultures' customs and laws can be made by outsiders? Those who stop at the conclusion that "a *nomos* is a *nomos*" and that nothing more can be said about it may have missed another layer to Herodotus' inquiry. As a good empiricist, Herodotus continued to collect data from around the world in order to see for himself whether there were any transcultural values concerning the nature of human being and what might constitute an Aristotelian-type notion of "human flourishing." The *Histories* is not, I think, a document which aims to present a foregone conclusion about cultural relativism. If that were so, it would not so successfully express Herodotus' driving sense of curiosity about and aliveness towards otherness. He is an investigator, an inquirer, not a mere recorder of difference. Herodotus scholar Donald Lateiner has remarked,

> but even the relativist cultural anthropologist or historian can define and judge otherness only from the standpoint of his own education and culture. Such evaluations have little worth if they are reached in a manner either condescending or unaware of a functional approach to human institutions.[6]

While we can strive to overcome our parochialism, we cannot avoid using our own heritage as a benchmark from which to discuss the success and failure, indeed, the humanity, of other cultures' practices. One can recognize one's cultural rootedness without completely giving up on the continuing inquiry into the nature of the human beneath the disguises of custom.

Herodotus never completely disavows Hellenic standards–sex with goats not only makes him flinch, but leads to his committing himself to a judgment that it is monstrous. While trying to "understand the world in less insular and parochial terms,"[7] Herodotus nonetheless makes commitments *within* relativism. He is not an absolute relativist. He is committed to a moral distinction between human beings and animals, no matter what he has observed in Egypt. But this commitment on his part only emerges after he has broken the broader taboos and confines of his own origins and *seen with his own eyes*. Herodotus' wide-sweeping views, openness, and deep imagination perhaps offer us a model for understanding ourselves and others in a period of moral and social disorientation.

From the viewpoint of our sophisticated historiography today, Herodotus' shortcomings are numerous: inconsistency, errors of fact and of judgment, weak chronology, acceptance of unreliable sources of information, and even, it has been suggested, deliberate falsehoods! However, more powerful than his technical historical method is his more general theory of inquiry. This consists of, first, breaking cultural taboos in order to see for oneself what is not one's own; and second, paying careful attention to, and analyzing, one's own reactions to this otherness. His so-called "cultural motives" may be complex; nonetheless, he *tries* to bring his own values and unconscious biases to the surface. He *tries* to insert a gap between experience and meaning, however impossible that may actually be. His attempt to "pull back" from the inference or interpretation of what he experiences shows us that, to a limited extent, he recognized that as a historian and ethnographer he was an active producer of knowledge and not merely a passive reporter.

How did this method of doing history display itself in our classroom? As students sought to interpret Herodotus' interpretations–in this case, having to do with the story of the woman and the goat–they became aware of our cultural taboo against sex with animals (Madonna's *Sex* book notwithstanding!) and analyzed their own "oh, yuk!" reactions. This led to an appreciation of the strong role of what appears to us as primitive religious ritual in an ancient culture.

Clearly, Herodotus was deeply interested in the relative nature of moral and cultural standards; however, he also recognized that one cannot observe others without reference to one's own culture. The students, too, recognized that we cannot understand Herodotus' storytelling without reference to the deep differences between ancient Greece and modern America in regard to the role of religion in everyday life. Is

Tradition and Innovation

this a profound insight in the classroom? Perhaps not. And yet it is one which is not so easily attained. We each struggle to see and understand "what is not our own" both within and beyond our cultural confines. Herodotus offers us a method for doing so, and by practicing this method we acquire two things at once: tolerance for others and a deeper appreciation of our own values and standards.

Notes

1. Seth Benardete, *Herodotean Inquiries* (The Hague: Martinus Nijhoff, 1969), 12-14; 23.

2. K. H. Waters, *Herodotus the Historian: His Problems, Methods and Originality* (University of Oklahoma Press, 1985), 34.

3. Alan B. Lloyd, *Herodotus Book II: Introduction* (Leiden, Netherlands: E. J. Brill, 1975), 81.

4. According to Alan B. Lloyd, scholars have found

> a strong tradition of bestiality in the Mendesain Nome and there is some evidence that the tradition is correct; for a mould has been found in the vicinity of Mendes which represents bestiality between a woman and a goat and there is proof of its currency in the Near and Far East as a cult act...Note that in order to obtain fertility women often exposed themselves in the presence of the sacred animal.

See his *Herodotus Book II: Commentary 1-98* (Leiden, Netherlands: E. J. Brill, 1975), 216.

5. Benardete, op.cit., 13.

6. Donald Lateiner, *The Historical Method of Herodotus* (Toronto: University of Toronto Press, 1989), 145.

7. Ibid.

The Relation of Tradition to Judgment

David E. Johnson

United States Naval Academy

How would you design a course in ethics to contribute to the character development (moral improvement) of eighteen- to twenty-two-year-old women and men? Why did we try to do it? Because part of the mission of the Naval Academy is the moral development of midshipmen and because the Navy in general and the Naval Academy in particular have been brought to public attention by a series of immoral/illegal acts by its students and recent graduates. Today I want to share with you the design and implementation of a new required core course in ethics, established fully for the first time in the fall of 1996. Traditional perspectives in philosophy have been brought to bear on perceived changes in the culture of the eighteen-year-olds entering our school (with concomitant changes in the culture of the school itself). The Naval Academy celebrated its one hundred fiftieth anniversary this past year, and the judgment has been that the traditional curriculum and way of doing things is sorely defective in the present circumstances.

This response to perceived moral problems among students is neither new nor unique to the Naval Academy. In 1977 a cheating scandal at the U.S. Military Academy at West Point led to the installation of a required core ethics course in the curriculum. Prior to that, starting in the early 1960s, Prof. Malham Wakin had pioneered the development of ethics instruction at the U.S. Air Force Academy.

What were the problems which led to the Navy's focus an ethics? During the Iran Contra hearings, Lt. Col. Oliver North, an infamous alumnus of Annapolis, claimed that he had not studied ethics at the Naval Academy. In particular, his behavior seemed to indicate a major lack of awareness of the U.S. Constitution as a behavioral guideline. Under pressure from Congress, the Naval Academy instituted a required course in the American constitution, as well as a program called "The Ethics Continuum" (a type of ethics across the curriculum). In this program, humanities and social science core courses were identified which hopefully contribute to the moral development of midshipmen. These included two semesters of Freshman English, two semesters of the history of Western Civilization, a political science course in the U.S. Constitution, and three courses in leadership. With minimal coordination among the departments involved, the administration hoped that these courses would teach "values" and improve the behavior of the midshipmen. This program, initiated in 1990, is still in place.

In December 1992, the Naval Academy experienced massive cheating in a required sophomore electrical engineering course. The investigation and resolution of this issue continued until the end of the summer, 1994, with regular headlines bringing the Academy into public question. One conclusion reached by naval leadership in the light of this cheating scandal was that the Ethics Continuum was not sufficient for moral education. Two additional steps were taken. First, the establishment of a division of character development that organized monthly ninety-minute discussion seminars for the entire student body. Second, the design and implementation of a required core ethics course. This second task was placed in the hands of an interdisciplinary faculty committee in order to focus on academic rigor rather than another training sequence. The focus was to be the study of core texts in philosophy. During the 1995-6 academic year a pilot version of the course was tested. Additional faculty were hired and the course was first taught as a required core course for the sophomore class in the fall of 1996.

Since our staff does not include ready-made the military counterpart of Plato's philosopher king, we found it necessary to grow our own military faculty by taking senior military officers and providing them with a quick course in philosophy. In both summers 1995 and 1996 the philosophy faculty conducted sixteen two-hour seminars (two a week for eight weeks) on: (1) the philosophical ethics materials contained in the course; (2) how to lead discussions of these texts rather than talk about them; and (3) how to lead a lively discussion of a case study. During the summer of 1996, topic (2) was presented by Dean Eva Brann of St. John's College, which specializes in discussions of the core texts of western civilization. Dean Brann is one of the preeminent practitioners of this approach. The philosophers on the team modeled the facilitation of discussion desired in the officers when they conduct their discussion sections. These seminars also provided opportunity for feedback from the officers on the length and difficulty of the readings. Based on this feedback, some of the readings were modified or deleted while others were left intact. This seminar approach to educating the officer instructors continued during the academic year around the course structure of one large lecture section (fifty to eighty midshipmen) and two small discussion sections (fifteen to twenty midshipmen) per week. On a Monday-Wednesday-Friday calendar, the lecture comes on Monday, followed by a seminar for the instructors on Monday or Tuesday. This seminar covers the readings for the week, possible teaching approaches to the material, and assessments of the effect of the previous week. The general pattern is for the officers to meet with the professor whose lectures they attend.

At present, our course integrates philosophical and ethical theory with practical applications in a military and military education context. The Monday lectures on ethical theory are discussed in small groups on Wednesday and applied to the cases discussed on Friday. The case and issue discussions take a variety of forms including debates and role plays. The marriage between theory and application is still an uneasy one at Annapolis. The students and many of the instructors are clamoring for "relevance" or "application." The philosophers stress that you need to have something to apply in order to engage in application. This debate is at least as old as Plato and Aristotle's dispute over the focus on reason as opposed to habituation in moral education. How do we assess what the course is doing? Some of us cringe at the possibility that when the big cheating scandal of 1999 hits the Naval Academy, we will be confronted by critics of the course asking "why didn't it [the required core ethics course] work?" Does a course in moral reasoning have a demonstrable impact on the moral behavior of students? Can right lecturing lead to right thinking and then to right acting on the part of the hearers? If so, what is the connection between right thought and right action? Should we reasonably expect that the incidents of lying, cheating and stealing will decrease at the Naval Academy once an ethics course has been established? Is reduced wrong-doing the measure of this course? On the face of it these questions seem wrong-headed. Our modest goals involve improving the midshipmen's moral rhetoric and skills in moral reasoning.

We have done regular and widespread evaluation of the course in several ways. First, approximately one-third to one-half of the students submit weekly electronic assessment from their own PCs to a set of questions. The midshipmen can and do add narrative comments to these evaluations. Another group of students from the same section then submit evaluations the following week, and the process continues all semester with this alternation. Those responses are tabulated and made available to the faculty in the course on Monday of the next week. At the end of the semester, the cumulative results of this process are summarized and analyzed. Second, during the weekly seminars for the instructors, the lecturers and instructors assess the previous week's readings (how well did they work to generate a lively discussion), lectures, and techniques employed in the small sections. At the end of the semester there is a separate session to evaluate the entire semester and propose changes for the readings and procedures in the next semester. Third, the students submit an end-of-course critique (the more customary type of college-level evaluation) providing a global review of their experience in the course. Our students are not shy about saying what they think of the course, both pro and con, so a fairly detailed representation of the course emerges.

So, how can we tell whether the course makes a difference in the daily lives of our students? Our evidence at present is anecdotal. Two papers are assigned during the semester, one on the lessons to be learned from the Tailhook incident, and the other on how the ethical positions studied can be applied to the midshipman's own relationship to members of the lower class whom he is responsible for training. The officers who supervise the students in the dormitory training environment report that they are beginning to see a difference between those who have taken the course and those who have not. In what respects? First, in how the male midshipmen deal with their female colleagues, that is, in engaging in less harassment. Second, in treating the freshmen (plebes) with greater respect for their dignity.

The Core Text

To support this course, we developed a core text, *Readings in Philosophy and Ethics for Naval Leaders*. This is synchronized with the syllabus and used in conjunction with several paperbacks in order to cover all the topics that we want to include. Because this course is a survey of major ethical theories and their application to a military context, we use major portions of Aristotle's *Nicomachean Ethics* and Kant's *Groundwork of the Metaphysics of Morals*. Otherwise we use shorter selections of material from Plato, Aquinas, Hobbes, Locke, Rousseau, the Bible, etc. With Kant we focus on the first two formulations of the categorical imperative. Of special interest in an organization that is hierarchical is the notion of autonomy built into all the formulations. In an organization that has trouble integrating women and which is built around the concept "enemy," we stress the importance of human dignity contained in the second formulation. Can that dignity and the rights that it undergirds be forfeited? Under what conditions?

We are trying to utilize traditional texts in a highly tradition-bound organization to awaken and sharpen the ability of our students to make moral judgments, i.e., to have a basis on which to distinguish good from bad, right from wrong. Although there is currently a lot of controversy in academe in general and philosophy in particular about the consequences of the Enlightenment in our culture, we live in a country whose institutions and procedures are the result of Enlightenment thinking. We see this course as promoting the use of reasoning in ethics in the hope of reducing some of the evil in the world.

How to Build a Learning Community:

Activate, Abdicate, Articulate

John A. Black

Malaspina University-College

Introduction

In this paper I want to offer practical suggestions for building a successful learning community. My comments have two sources: first, my experience teaching in the Liberal Studies B.A. program at Malaspina University-College and, second, the notion of community developed by Aristotle in the *Nicomachean Ethics*. My over-simplistic formula for success is this: activate, abdicate, articulate. I hope that in the detail of my remarks, as in my pedagogical practice, there will be sufficient complexity to exonerate me of the charges of glibness and an undue devotion to the formulaic.

A word or two first about the circumstances of the Malaspina program: unlike many–perhaps St. John's is a good example–Malaspina is not a residential college. Many of our students are part-time, and all take elective courses outside the core program, which occupies sixty percent of their load in third and fourth year. They join the program having developed most of their academic skills and expectations in two years of traditional lecture classes. Most work while they attend college, and a good number have responsibilities as parents. Furthermore, Nanaimo, British Columbia is relatively impoverished as a center of (Euro-Canadian, at least) culture, so that students do not experience the kind of extramural intellectual community-building which, for example, was a major part–perhaps *the* major part–of my undergraduate education at the University of Cambridge. In a context of this sort, it becomes necessary to devote specific attention to developing a learning community, since circumstances conspire to prevent it appearing of its own accord.

As I see it, a learning community is such in two senses: it is a community which promotes learning, and it is also a community which must itself learn–among other things, to be a learning community. This reification of the community as a subject of learning is not idle, and does not overlook the dependence of community learning upon individual learning: rather, it serves to emphasize the importance of creating and maintaining a culture of community reliance. Students must believe, like Aristotle, that they are *essentially* members of a community. For this to happen in a college, and to avoid tokenistic attitudes toward the ideal of a learning community, requires that the students and faculty become friends in a real sense. And there are many ways in which faculty can design a pedagogy to promote a kind of friendship which is manifest in academic activity. At Malaspina, for example, students hold tutorials without faculty supervision in order to evaluate preliminary drafts of essays, and are sometimes asked to evaluate the seminar participation of their peers. Certain assignments, especially projects in art or science, are completed by small groups, all members of a group receiving the same mark. It is even possible to work the conception of a community being itself a subject of learning into course content. While investigating the use of averaging in scientific measurement, for example, we asked students to estimate the age of one of the faculty. While individual results ranged five years on either side of the true value, the group average was correct to within three weeks!

If a learning community, then, must be a community of friends, there are other ways in which course content can be suborned in the service of this ideal. Because our program proceeds chronologically from the Old Testament and the Greeks, it is about halfway through the first term that we come to Aristotle, and reading the *Nicomachean Ethics* provides the perfect opportunity for discussing notions of community and encouraging some self-application of the concept. This brings me to the first element of my slogan:

Activate
One of Aristotle's ideas with which our students often disagree is his remark that true friends must live together. They take it to mean, of course, that friends must share houses or apartments, and to this they are loth to commit, reserving, as true individualists, the option of their "own space." I take it, however, that Aristotle was not primarily inter-

ested in co-op housing, and that his point, derived from the familiar notion that good living is *activity* (*energeia*), is that friendship must be exercised in collaborative activity which manifests both moral and intellectual virtue. This claim has consequences for learning community pedagogy.

It ties that pedagogy, to begin with, to the idea of active learning. This is not a new idea, but it is worth mentioning all the same, since its implementation is required by the defining assumption of our interdisciplinary program, that the main goal, again eminently Aristotelian, is to enhance students' general intellectual skills, for example in communication, critical thinking and cultural awareness, rather than to instill knowledge peculiar to a discipline. The practical suggestions relevant here are to avoid over-reliance on lectures, to prefer seminar discussion in which active participation is a requirement, and to include class activities, such as science labs and art studios, which place on students a wide variety of demands for active involvement. We have had great success at Malaspina in incorporating elements of fine and performing arts: mask-making workshops, group painting and sculpture projects, play-readings, dance, music, singing, video production and so on. Such academically "adventurous" activities provide an opportunity for limited intellectual heroism and pioneer spirit, as do simple field trips through the northern snow to visit an observatory or underground cavern. They contribute to the building of community in two ways: first, through shared experience and creative activity where the demands are academically unfamiliar, and therefore risky; second, through community celebration of individual contribution and performance, whether in presenting a skit or driving the bus. They require and, therefore, promote a high level of trust, which spills over into other activities such as peer evaluation and seminar participation. An educational bonus which some, but not all, faculty have failed to anticipate is that the creative arts components greatly enrich the more traditional academic work, in discussion and writing, which forms the greater part, still, of student activity.

Abdicate

Furthermore, if a community is to be truly focused on active learning, it is necessary for faculty to redefine their roles in relation to students. Traditional roles, such as that of the fountain of truth, which encourage student passivity, as well as an over-reliance on authority, must be abandoned if room is to be left for the expansion of student activity. One must undermine expectations that faculty are the sole controllers of both the learning process and the injection of content. Instead, students must come to take themselves seriously as autonomous sources of ideas and perspectives, as sites of methodological and even pedagogical expertise, and as participants responsible to some degree for the encouragement and success of their peers. As Aristotle says, the true friend takes his friend's goals as his own. There are various ways in which this shift of the onus of responsibility for content, skill-development and motivation can be achieved. I shall mention a couple of examples.

First, there is team-teaching. The multiplicity of perspectives represented in a closely-knit team of faculty goes a long way towards undermining the notions of the professor as semi-divine authority, or as commander-in-chief of the learning process. In addition, such a team can, in the interaction of its members, do much to model learning community virtues such as a respectful demeanor in seminar discussion, how to handle rational disagreement, and so on. A faculty team will be most successful, I suggest, if it engages in the active learning "adventures" described earlier in the same way, and on the same level, as students. Not only will this include faculty in the general spirit of camaraderie, it will also define them as members of the *same* learning community as the students, and not of an elite group set apart.

Second, the faculty member must try to avoid being always the center of attention, especially in seminars. It goes without saying that in classes of this type the point is to facilitate, not to lecture. Yet even students who adopt an active and leading role in discussion may, as a result of the more traditional contexts in which they have acquired their educational habits, direct most of their comments to the professor. This is particularly disturbing when the comment is a reply to one previously made by another student. A simple expedient, but one which it is not easy to adopt without conscious effort, is to break eye-contact with the responder and look towards the source of the original remark. This will usually have the desired effect of deflecting the responder's attention to its proper object.

Two general qualifications must be made at this point: first, I'm not of course suggesting a total abandonment of all responsibility on the part of faculty, just a shift of emphasis towards a willingness to share the responsibility in a way which promotes skill development among students; second, it is of vital importance that when such a shift occurs, it does so because it has been adopted in full sincerity by the faculty involved. Mere lip-service to educational democracy will be seen by students to be exactly that, and will backfire with destructive consequences for the learning community.

Articulate

The last of my triad of pedagogical injunctions concerns the need to make absolutely clear to students the shift in pedagogical strategy and the resulting changes in the expectations placed upon them. I speak from unpleasant personal experience here. Despite repeated announcements in promotional material that the program involved student-centered active learning, the first team I coordinated in Liberal Studies was met with a torrent of student complaints during its first term. When we tried "outsider" lectures à la Meiklejohn, we were told we didn't know our subject; when we refrained from controlling the content of seminars, we were told we were poor facilitators and shirkers of the professorial duty to pontificate. Our students had not made any adjustment in their traditional expectations, and did not realize that we had adopted a different approach to pedagogy. Our best efforts to explain, belatedly, what we were up to met with a skepticism which did not entirely dissipate over the remaining year and a half we spent with that group. Needless to say, we made quite sure with our second intake, through an intensive week of orientation, that they understood exactly why the approach was different, and exactly what the implications were for the roles both they and faculty were expected to fulfill. Taking the students through this orientation enabled us to gain greater clarity on our own pedagogical strategies, and probably led to greater consistency in their implementation. It certainly had the effect of forestalling the kind of negative reaction we had experienced the first time.

Summary

My point in this short paper has been this: the best way to enhance the development of general intellectual skills is through *building a learning community*; to create the most effective learning community, it is necessary to *activate* students in their educational experiences and endeavors; to maximize their level of active involvement in learning, it is necessary to *abdicate* the professor's traditional role as classroom monarch; and to modify this role sufficiently without running afoul of the traditional expectations of students, it is necessary to *articulate* the nature and justification of the pedagogical shift you have made.

The Analytic Essay:

Teaching Writing in an Interdisciplinary Course

Marsha L. Dutton[*]

Hanover College

The single surviving Old English epic, *Beowulf*, begins with a prologue introducing the fabled ancestor of the Danes, Scyld Scefing. In its
mythical description of Scyld's origins, life, death, and sea-burial, this
prologue explicitly defines good kingship:

> Attend!
> We have heard of the thriving of the throne of Denmark,
> how the folk-kings flourished in former days,
> how those royal athelings earned that glory.
> Was it not Scyld Scefing that shook the halls,
> took mead-benches, taught encroaching
> foes to fear him—who, found in childhood,
> lacked clothing? Yet he lived and prospered,
> grew in strength and stature under the heavens
> until the clans settled in the sea-coasts neighboring
> over the whale-road all [had to] obey him
> and give tribute. He was a good king!
> A boy child was afterwards born to Scyld,
> a young child in hall-yard, a hope for the people,
> sent them by God.[1]

(1-15)

At the end of the epic the elderly Geatish king Beowulf, who in his youth came to the aid of the monster-ridden descendants of Scyld, fights with a dragon over the dragon's hoard, killing and being killed by the dragon. He leaves no heir. The work concludes, ambiguous as the prologue is didactic, as his people grieve around his tomb:

> A woman of the Geats in grief sang out
> the lament for his death. Loudly she sang,
> her hair bound up, the burden of her fear
> that evil days were destined her
> —troops cut down, terror of armies,
> bondage, humiliation. Heaven swallowed the smoke.
> . . . .
> Then the warriors rode around the barrow,
> twelve of them in all, athelings' sons.
> They recited a dirge to declare their grief,
> spoke of the man, mourned their King.
> They praised his manhood and the prowess of his hands,
> they raised his name.
> . . . .
> This was the manner of the mourning of the men of the Geats,
> sharers in the feast, at the fall of their lord:
> they said that he was of all the world's kings
> the gentlest of men, and the most gracious,
> the kindest to his people, the keenest for fame.
>
> (3150-5, 3168-73, 3178-82)

The question raised by these concluding lines, and therefore by the epic as a whole, is this: Was Beowulf a good king? The defining structure, which suggests the epic to be almost an early mirror for princes, leaves the reader unsure. He does much of what Scyld does, but he fails to leave a son. And while his warriors acclaim him at his death as gentle, gracious, kind, and keen for fame, the grieving woman proclaims the disaster that his keenness for fame and greed for treasure have brought to his people. How does one resolve the conflict between her grief and that of the warriors? Or is their grief perhaps also an acknowledgment that the possession of gentleness, graciousness, kindness, and keenness for fame is not finally enough for good kingship unless one leaves an heir to protect the people?

With such questions the twelve Hanover College faculty members who teach the freshman-sophomore core course, "Eurasia: Science and the Humanities," guide students to explore works of literature, art, history, political theory, theology, and natural science and to learn to write analytic essays about the meaning of those works. This interdisciplinary course invites students and faculty to join together in inquiry into the intellectual, cultural, and political history of China, Japan, and the West through examination of primary documents and artifacts. The recent addition of writing to the course's curriculum has broadened the experience and understanding of both students and faculty. While we have begun by focusing on ways of teaching writing as one of the subjects of the course rather than merely using it for evaluation of other subjects, we seek also to use it as a means of inquiry, an enhancement of rational thought, imaginative exploration, and travel toward wisdom.

Eurasia, which explores the history, art, and thought of the world, East and West, from their beginnings through the present, originated in 1992 as the vision of Hanover's then-dean of the college, Charles L. Flynn, Jr. The program was in part a response to the college's expanded General Degree Requirements. Part of the initial resistance of some faculty against approving these new requirements resulted from anxiety that students would be left with too little room for electives; the creation of interdisciplinary courses that satisfied multiple requirements satisfactorily answered that concern. From its beginnings Eurasia allowed students in three terms—essentially three courses—to satisfy six General Degree Requirements, those in literature, history, fine arts, theology, philosophy, and non-Western history and culture. In 1995 the Eurasia faculty reshaped the course, eliminating theology and philosophy in response to the wish of those departments and adding components to satisfy GDRs in the natural sciences and the analytic essay. To distinguish the new course from the old we renamed it "Eurasia: Science and the Humanities."

In the course of each three-term cycle twelve faculty participate actively in Eurasia, four having particular responsibility each term. Students meet five days a week, ideally three days in fifteen-person discussion sections and two in sixty-person lectures. Each term's faculty cooperate in planning, teaching, reviewing, and revising that term's course.

Introducing the GDR of the Analytic Essay to the program has been exhilarating for the Eurasia faculty, only two of whom have ever before taught (rather than assigning and grading) writing. While most of the non-English faculty in the program require extensive writing of all their students, evaluating the papers they receive thoughtfully, commenting carefully on both structure and style, and sometimes requiring students to submit major papers in introductory stages in order that they may give early feedback and counsel, only Eurasia's two English professors have spent class time teaching the rudiments of formal argumentative writing. Our chemist said as we began to shape the first year's approach, "You mean we would spend a whole hour talking just about how to write? I never even thought about what people *did* in writing classes!"

Not surprisingly, the two English professors have so far been not only heading up the writing component of the course but also, along the way, teaching our colleagues how to teach writing. Although the approach has worked well during this first year, we plan next August (before the third course of the first cycle and the first course of the second cycle) to conduct a day-long workshop during which we can instruct one another and ensure that all who teach the course are equally competent and confident in teaching and grading student writing.

Our fundamental approach in this first year of incorporating writing into Eurasia has been to schedule one writing workshop for each week of each term, meeting sometimes in lecture (that is, with all sixty students and four faculty meeting together) and sometimes in the discussion sections. In the first of these workshops I led the students in a discussion of the steps of writing: preparation, the role of thinking and planning and even just strolling around playing with ideas, and some approaches to overcoming the difficulty of getting first thoughts down on paper, including free-writing, lists of ideas, or an e-mail to a friend exploring ideas, possible structures, and anticipated problems. That first day we barely mentioned the essay itself, concentrating instead on encouraging students to talk about their own ways of beginning, of organizing, and of writing. We talked openly about how hard writing is and why it is so hard, and we considered the necessity of such steps as warming up, practicing, and developing a kind of muscle memory for formal writing. One faculty member, a classicist, commented afterward that the process of beginning by inviting students to discuss their own writing experiences "made writing seem like a human endeavor."

Each week for two terms we have followed this approach, teaching writing by inviting students to bring their own experiences, insights, abilities, problems, habits, and questions to the center of the discussion. We give staged assignments, always asking students to submit each stage of each paper at least twice, in order that we may give response and guidance along the way rather than only a grade at the end. Our fundamental goal in this respect is to *teach* writing rather than merely to grade it, to assist students in learning how to do this terribly difficult thing one small step at a time. In both sections and lecture we focus on the thesis sentence that controls the paper, on paragraphs and the topic sentences that control them, on key words, on the use and citation of evidence. We move from a brief examination of one work or idea to a comparison of two or three ideas or authors or works and then to papers involving secondary research. We comment, ask questions, point to structural difficulties and successes. We try hard to praise as much as criticize, always to give specific direction and help rather than merely an unexplained grade.

The subject matter of our writing is, of course, the substance of the course. In the second week of the term, after the discussion sections had discussed *Beowulf,* I again led the whole group in a writing workshop, beginning with the question about kingship posed by the work's structure, asking students in the tiered auditorium where we meet to debate the related issues, supporting their points with evidence, in response to the question "Was Beowulf a good king?" After about ten minutes of discussion, with students offering a wide range of textual citations in support of their different positions, we stopped talking about the question itself and began instead to explore how one writes a paper on such a topic: raising a substantive question, analyzing resources to find an answer, presenting that answer as thesis of the paper, and developing a supporting argument for the thesis from the evidence that led there in the first place. We talked about the thesis sentence as essentially argumentative, emerging from analysis and evidence. It was a wonderful session, one that served as a basis for successive sessions exploring the primary documents and artifacts studied in the class and the method of developing argumentative papers from those sources.

The faculty meet together after every paper's due date to share the grading of a few papers from each discussion section, so that we can be sure that we are grading similarly and so that those of us who are accustomed to teaching writing can continue to help our colleagues. From time to time a colleague who is finding difficulty in grading a paper will bring it to one of the English professors for assistance, but each person always grades the papers from his or her own section.

We continue to experiment with ways to teach writing. One thing we do often is to use the writing workshop as a laboratory, a real workshop. There, students read each other's papers and consider their argument or evidence, evaluate thesis and topic sentences, and make suggestions for improvement. Sometimes we ask them to identify the best sentence or best paragraph on their partner's paper and, then, to explain why they chose that one. Other times, as a way to work on the use of concrete detail, we tell them to exchange papers and to read and, then, write three concrete questions on their partners' papers. After reading the questions on their own papers, they are asked to add two more concrete questions. We always tell students what to consider in such workshops so that they can focus their efforts precisely.

Students consistently respond seriously and conscientiously to the opportunity this approach gives of assisting one another. On the day the first draft of their first paper was due last fall, we asked each one to glance through someone else's paper to catch grammatical errors and comment on stylistic or structural problems that the writer might work on in the revision stage. As our intention was merely to point out the necessity of proofreading and to continue the practice of peer editing, we expected the result to be not much more than a few corrected misspellings. Instead, all the papers came in heavily marked, corrected, and annotated, with thesis sentences rewritten, paragraphs rearranged, and new evidence inserted. The students had understood our instructions as serious ones, and they responded accordingly. The result was that when we read their first drafts we were able to respond not only to what the writers had brought to class but to their initial revisions.

While continuing to use this workshop approach, the faculty teaching the second term of Eurasia added some different and still more focused exercises. As a way of understanding correct citation form and the various misuses of evidence that constitute plagiarism, Dr. Dee Goertz on a Monday passed out a worksheet with a passage from a secondary source followed by four paragraphs paraphrasing or quoting that source. Each paragraph was followed by a space for students to evaluate the use and citation of the evidence. On Wednesday, when the students brought their completed worksheet to the lecture, she spent ten minutes at the beginning of the hour talking with them about the advantages, disadvantages, and faults of each form of quotation and citation. It was an effective way to explain quotation and citation style and to warn against plagiarism, always a difficult area for college freshmen.

In addition to asking students to work closely with the process of writing and revising, we keep experimenting with new ways to encourage conversation between student writers and professors, trying to maintain a conversation about their writing not only before they write and as they write but even after they have completed and submitted a paper. On each first draft submitted we ask students to provide a cover page listing only an outline of the thesis and topic sentences; we initially focus our comments on that page rather than allowing ourselves to be distracted by grammatical and stylistic matters. We ask that they submit papers in cardboard folders with all notes and earlier drafts included so that we can check the origins of their ideas and phrases and comment on improvements between the draft and the finished version.

We ask that on the back of both the original and the final versions they write their own evaluation of one or two aspects of the paper: sometimes their thesis or topic sentences, sometimes their use of evidence–whatever we have been concentrating on in the previous weeks. And we ask them to grade their papers provisionally on the basis of that evaluation, with comments. We often also ask them to write on the back of the first draft identifying problems to which they would like us to give particular attention, and on the back of the final draft we ask them to say what they would do if they had more time to work on the paper. When handing back the final version we ask them to read our comments and respond in writing. We do everything we can to teach them how to write, personally, interactively, humanely. And we find that by so doing we better teach the substance of the course as well.

Was Beowulf a good king? The Eurasia class discussion of that question was stimulating, wide ranging, and dynamic. Students took positions, supported them with evidence, and argued with one another. They discovered that they could care passionately about a literary question, and they discovered that literature of the past concerned issues they could understand. By the time the class was over, they had also learned to define an argumentative thesis, to identify logical steps in an argument, and to recognize evidence both for and against their own position. They had learned that their opinion was what we sought to hear, but that we wanted to know not only what they thought but on what basis. They had begun to learn how to construct a reasoned argument and how to write it down. They had begun to be writers.

Note

1. *Beowulf,* trans. Michael Alexander (New York: Penguin, 1973).

Interpretations

Tocqueville and Liberal Education

William Mathie

Brock University

The purposes of the Association for Core Texts and Courses I have supposed to be the promotion of liberal education and the use of what are here designated core texts in that education–"core texts" I take to be a politically correct way of speaking of what others call "great books." Our aim in this panel and my own aim in this paper is to identify the special merits of Tocqueville's *Democracy in America* within this larger purpose.

Following a long tradition, I take a liberal education to be an education that makes us free, where freedom is understood in contrast to a condition of slavery. The slavery from which liberal education frees us is above all the slavery of opinions, whether those opinions be those into which we have been born as members of a particular class or race or sex or those that are most insisted upon explicitly or implicitly by our society and its rulers. The freedom toward which liberal education aims has as its motto the words of Socrates, who may be the founder of liberal education partly because these are his words: the unexamined life is not worth living. Socrates has also furnished what has often been taken as a powerful image of liberal education in the picture he paints in the seventh book of Plato's *Republic*. Socrates describes us there as prisoners in a cave who can only see shadows and hear echoes. The shadows we see upon the wall of the cave are cast by artifacts carried by strange puppeteers who move behind us but in front of a fire, and the echoes we hear are made by those same puppeteers. The prisoners are deprived of any awareness that they inhabit a cave, that there exists any reality but the shadows on the wall and the echoes they hear. They have seen nothing even of themselves or their fellows other than the shadows on the wall. Such is Socrates' image of "our nature in its education and want of education." As for liberal education, in terms of this image we must suppose it to mean awareness that the cave is a cave, that the shadows are merely shadows cast by the puppeteers; and perhaps it allows us finally to escape from that cave to discover the truth outside. As for its means, Socrates leaves this shrouded in mystery, but he does suggest that escaping from the world of images is immensely difficult, that we must be dragged from our imprisonment "kicking and screaming."

Now if we are prisoners of the kind Socrates describes, the cave we inhabit must be that of democracy. But here is a paradox. If liberal education aims at freedom, so does democracy. Freedom is the principle of democracy according to Socrates himself. Democracy is the regime characterized by freedom both because it overthrows the mean-spiritedness of oligarchy and because it is the regime in which an immense variety of lives become available to us–and even a variety within our lives as we pursue one, rather than another, choice. And we are inclined to say that if democracy is a good thing and liberal education is a good thing the two must be compatible, if not synonymous. (Just as our students want to say, "Democracy is a good thing; Socrates was a good man; Socrates was a democrat.") So, at the very least, we want to say that liberal education serves the cause of democracy. And perhaps it does, but we should be wary lest our enthusiasm for liberal education and our dislike of inequality, or even our concern that liberal education survive and flourish in our own world, lead us to assume just what we ought to question.

If Tocqueville's *Democracy in America* can help us and our students escape from the cave of democracy, it is partly because he forces us to rethink the simple equation of democracy and liberal education.[1] From its first to its last pages *Democracy in America* is constructed around the opposition between the equality of social conditions that increasingly characterizes modernity and defines democracy for Tocqueville, on the one hand, and, on the other, the various forms of social inequality found in all previous societies that Tocqueville gathers together under the name aristocracy. The distinction between democracy and aristocracy is the key to understanding politics for Tocqueville and it seems also to be the fundamental fact about the human condition (3, 677).[2] And it is the ambiguity and complexity we encounter as we see and reflect upon what we find on the opposing sides of this distinction that make *Democracy in America* so important a text within a liberal education.

A preliminary, if hasty, way of trying to capture some of this ambiguity would be to say that what we see in Tocqueville's analysis is that beauty and excellence in the arts–in craftsmanship as well as in the fine arts like poetry–and several of the virtues, like generosity, belong to aristocracy, while truth and certainly justice are favored by democracy (432-4). And this in itself might provide a solid reason for valuing what we and our students can learn from Tocqueville.[3] And yet even the case of truth proves far from simple when we reflect upon Tocqueville's argument. Democracy favors the truth as does liberal education, we might say, for it approximates the Cartesian principle of judging everything for oneself; whereas in aristocracy our opinions are those of our ancestors or our class (393). Aristocracy in its classic expression is based upon hereditary wealth in land, so the inequality it maintains is utterly arbitrary; moreover, what makes sense of the aristocratic notion of inheritance is the "illusion" that we can make ourselves immortal through our posterity (46). The falseness of aristocratic society is even more manifest in the instance of the servant who identifies with his master so completely as to lose his very self (550). And yet a society based upon the truth–the truth about human nature–and free from illusion may not favor the pursuit of truth. This is something Tocqueville both shows and explains. Democracy forces us to judge all things for ourselves but it cannot make us capable of doing so; all societies and individuals must rely upon dogmatic opinions most of the time (398-400). The only question is where we get those opinions. Democracy makes each of us unwilling to acknowledge the intellectual authority of any other human being. If no human being is any wiser than any other, all that can distinguish one opinion from another is how many share it. Public opinion, the opinion of the majority, becomes the sole and absolute source of dogma. The denial of the very idea of the intellectual superior shuts each of us up inside ourselves so as to make inaccessible any notion of truth or beauty. On this account, liberal democracy is hardly the home of liberal education. It is rather a cave within which each of us as an individual is the prisoner of all of us as we make up the opinion of society.

Could one say that even if it is very precarious, nevertheless, liberal education is something liberal democracy needs? Certainly liberal democracy needs something. Though democracy as equality of social conditions is certain–the fate of the modern world–liberty is not, for it is threatened by the power of public opinion. But what preserves liberty is not liberal education but illusions like religion which can uphold limits to what even public opinion can do. And religion is as strong as it is in democratic society not because it is thought to be true, but because each of us thinks it is the opinion of most of us (400). Another famous safeguard of liberty according to Tocqueville is participation in the public life of democracy through association; but the analysis of democratic life from the perspective of liberal education as furnished by Tocqueville hardly encourages such involvement. Consider his description of "the gravity" of the wealthy American whose favorite entertainment is to quietly drink himself into a stupor at his own hearth (585). Or the explanation he gives of the marital fidelity of American men—they are too tired or too lacking in imagination to be guilty of adultery (573).

How then does *Democracy in America* serve the purposes of liberal education in democracy if what it teaches is this deep opposition between the two? One might argue that it does so precisely by revealing this tension, that we are freed to an extent by perceiving that the democratic regime is a cave after all. As students of Tocqueville, we and our students can learn how profoundly the democratic regime shapes our opinions and our lives. Beyond that, we are led perhaps to a chastening of all political hopes, for we learn that democracy which is our inescapable condition is the enemy of beauty and human excellence and even of the disinterested pursuit of truth, that aristocracy which favors those things is both unavailable and itself based on things that are arbitrary and illusory. It may well be that this chastening of political hope is the proper condition for liberal education. On the other hand, if this account of Tocqueville's teaching is at all accurate, one could raise two objections to that teaching. First, one could observe that if Tocqueville leads us to see that democracy is a cave, he does not lead us to see that we can ever escape from that cave.[4] In the second place, one might say that if public opinion in democracy is as enthralling as Tocqueville claims, it is curious that so many of us are able to be persuaded by his account. These reflections might lead us to conclude that what makes Tocqueville so valuable a text from the perspective of liberal education is not simply the answers it supplies but also, or more so, the questions it poses.

Notes

1. Patrick Malcolmson and Richard Myers have argued the value of Tocqueville in freeing students from the cave of the democratic regime by enabling them to see how much that regime restricts them through the utilitarianism and intellectual conformity it imposes upon them. See, for example, their "Liberal Education and Political Science," a paper presented to the May 1996 conference on "Liberal Arts and the Future of University Education" sponsored by the Centre for Interdisciplinary Research in the Liberal Arts at Banff.

2. References in parentheses are to the edition of J.P.Mayer and Max Lerner, *Democracy in America*, (New York: Harper and Row, 1966).

3 Something like this is argued by Peter Lawler in his recent essay, "Love, Death, and Liberal Education," *Gravitas*, Winter 1997, 28-33.

4. As Myers and Malcomson say, he "liberates us from the shackles but not from the cave" (8).

Comparative Ascents:

Plato's Allegory of the Cave and the Liberation of the Israelites from Slavery as Models for Core Education

George M. Gross

Felician College

In this presentation I would like to explore some of the benefits that may result from placing Plato's *Republic* before the Hebrew Bible in the sequence of readings in a core course focusing on antiquity. My own experience, and that of the students I have taught, is that the encounter with the Bible becomes fuller and richer. In the ordering that I describe, Plato's *Republic* functions as a propaedeutic and aids in disposing a reader to consider the Exodus account as depicting a recurrent and universal experience as well as a principally national one.

Placing Plato before the Bible is a reversal of the ordinary procedure that the Socratic dialectic seems to call for, in which the familiar should precede the strange or the foreign. Yet, to many of our students, and indeed to many teachers (and I do not entirely exempt myself), the Bible is as foreign as Plato. Whatever mileage one may think to gain by placing the Bible first in the sequence of readings is liable to be vitiated by the fact that many of our students, and even some of our teachers, have not read it before, and so it is not really familiar. There is, on the other hand, a danger that placing Plato first may elicit too Platonistic a reading of the Bible. Placing *The Republic* first may serve a unifying purpose, however. Because *The Republic* is more likely to be new and foreign or strange to everyone (or because, as Euclid teaches, the farther away a point is the longer it will take two lines that pass through it to intersect), *The Republic* supplies an opportunity to fashion a common reading experience at the beginning of a course where the first reading might otherwise be divisive.

These personal or autobiographical core readings of ours aim to bring about clarity, or knowledge, regarding opinion. They describe ascent, or liberation, from reigning opinions. The passages I comment on here deal thematically with the problem of ascent or liberation. The divided line in book six of *The Republic* works theoretically to structure the allegory of the cave. The allegory may do so in turn for a reading of Exodus. Whether such a reading does violence to the intention of Exodus is one question that motivates this presentation.

The allegory of the cave and Exodus present images of ascent from slavery to liberation. *The Republic* operates in the realm of philosophy and provides an example of the dialectic that it describes. Exodus seems to operate in the realm of history. Like pre-modern historical writings generally (such as Thucydides, the Gospels, or the West African epic *Sundiata*), it is history in the sense of moral interpretation. Even the order and the content of the episodes are subject to alteration for the sake of the teachings they convey. The accounts of the manna and the quails in Exodus and Numbers are examples. In Exodus, the quails precede the manna and the emphasis is on instructing the Israelites, preparing them to receive the law at Sinai. In Numbers, the manna precedes the quails and the emphasis is on the punishment of those who are rebellious and impatient. Each book treats each episode in accordance with its ruling purpose. Exodus focuses on the obdurateness of the people in the context of their inspiritment as a precondition to receiving the law, while Numbers indicates a generous typology of the rebellions that Moses has either to quell or accommodate, not all of which are in the nature of popular uprisings.

The goal of the journey that Exodus describes is the acceptance of law under the covenant. Exodus supplies a sustained consideration of the way of life according to law. For a people of slaves, accustomed to equate law with the caprice of tyranny under Pharaoh, the transformation is momentous. The problematic relation of man and law, law-abidingness as an attribute of man, is the theme here. The account of the Creation in Genesis teaches that man is the only creature that can transgress, but Exodus complements this teaching by contending that man is the only creature that can be heedful.

The allegory of the cave holds out the possibility of liberating a rare individual, Exodus, an entire people. Each uses the metaphor of stiff-neckedness as the starting point, the essential characteristic of slavery.

The prisoners in Plato's allegory are bound so that they cannot move their necks. The images they see flickering and passing before them are projections of natural and artificial compounds under human management. The cave is an artificial environment that mitigates the sense of man's transitoriness or dependence. In this climate there is a competition for glory and honors as those who are chained compete to predict the order of the flickering shadows. One prisoner is suddenly freed and passes painfully through a series of stages which are roughly assimilable to the levels of the divided line. At each stage he encounters images of images. The Sun, at which the freed man eventually comes to gaze, and on which everything depends, and which he is tempted to worship, is itself an image, the offspring of the Good, the supreme maker of images of itself.

In Plato's *Republic*, there are two descents to complement the freed man's singular ascent. This duality may be an acknowledgment of the autobiographical quality of Socrates' image of the freed man as well as a concession to the perplexity that the career of Socrates engenders. The first descent is like that of Socrates himself. In his exuberant return to the cave, the land of the ungrateful dead, the one who descends injudiciously reports his findings and is rapidly killed by his former comrade inmates. Here the allegory of the cave merges overtly with Plato's *Apology of Socrates*.

The thwarting of the first descent supplies the occasion for Socrates to advance the theory of education as the turning of the soul, the inculcation of right habits, whose conditions include, as outlined in earlier books of *The Republic*, the requisite musical and physical education. The second descent is like that of Socrates, too, but it is also like that of Plato. The second descent qualifies and suppresses the mode of philosophy as liberation. In a reluctant and calibrated return to the cave, the one who descends parcels out, in parsimonious fashion, if at all, the discoveries he has made. In the second descent, the one who returns accustoms his eyes to seeing in the dark.

Exodus is also a compound of ascents and descents. The principal ascent is that of the stiff-necked Israelites from slavery to freedom. Moses' first effort to bring law and judgment to the Israelites ends in their seeking to kill him (Ex 2:14-15). Moses then leaves politics, or metaphorical shepherding. As a shepherd in Midian, Moses is not superstitious and has enough knowledge of natural science to recognize the odd occurrence of the burning bush, which he turns aside to investigate. In the dialogue that follows, Moses objects five times to the demand that he descend to execute the liberation of the Israelites. Since the arguments that he is given here are unpersuasive, Moses is finally compelled to go down by having his arm twisted (Ex 4:14-17). Thus the contumacy and the unwillingness of the partners seem perfectly matched. The people do not want to go up, and Moses does not want to go down. The journey of Moses to Mt. Sinai, the place where the law is to be given, precedes that of the Israelites and is a higher ascent than theirs.

The exodus from slavery in Egypt takes place in a series of stages or levels (Ex 17:1; Num 33:1-2). The internal logic of these stages defies the intuition of Pharaoh (and perhaps of many readers as well) that the Israelites are "wandering aimlessly" (Ex 14:3) in the wilderness. The overall structure of the narrative's grand frame–ten plagues, ten revolts in the wilderness (see Numbers 14:22), ten commandments–suggests a series of measured phases. Each phase must run its course before the next phase may begin. In the central phase, the series of revolts in the wilderness, a great revolution takes place.

Exodus describes the Israelites on the eve of Moses' appearance before them as "broken in spirit" (Ex 6:9) on account of their cruel slavery. The stages of their ascent (Ex 12:38) contribute to their inspiritment. Their journey follows a roundabout route because they are unwilling to fight when they pull out of Egypt (Ex 13:17-18). First, the Israelites are told to stand firm, indeed, to stand still. At the next level, they sing a song. Still later, they receive complicated instructions for gathering and preparing the manna, which they disobey, and so they need to be instructed again. The last act that prepares them to receive the law is the battle that they fight against Amalek. The battle with Amalek at the end of the wanderings sequence in Exodus (Ex 17:8-13) signifies the fashioning of the slaves into a people of courage and spirit, ready to accept (and to defend) the law under the covenant at Mt. Sinai. The climactic scene of Exodus is at Sinai, but its culminating moment is the unanimous freewill offering that the people contribute for making the things that go with the holy ark.

Perhaps the experience of the Israelites is similar to that of Crito, to whom Socrates has to make the case for obedience to the laws. In a democracy, the people make the laws, but in *Crito*, the laws contend in the speech that Socrates frames for them that they are the makers of men. Pharaoh's Egypt and the Athens of Crito are similar in that both regimes display a propensity to teach that the laws are artifices of men.

I began this presentation by asking whether reading Exodus in the light of Plato's teaching in *The Republic* may lend itself to inflicting a certain violence on the teaching of Exodus. One should also ask whether a reading of *The Republic* may be essential as a preparation for beginning to understand the Biblical teaching. Whether one reads Plato's *Republic* as an introduction to Exodus, or Exodus as an introduction to Plato, it seems useful to try to clarify the extent to which the domains of the two works may coincide in the centrality that each assigns to the theme of liberation as ascent.

"You Can(t) Teach Proust to Undergraduates"

Phillip Bailey

University of Central Arkansas

Marcel Proust's *In Search of Lost Time* ranks high on the list of any serious reader's literary canon. As such, Proust would seem to hold a secure place within the tradition of the reading of the "classics." And yet, there seems to be an increasing number of scholars whose gloomy pessimism concerning the attention span of the average late-twentieth-century high-school graduate would de facto relegate Proust and others to the dustbins of literary history and the margins of core curricular syllabi. The challenge raised in my title refers to the quip of a not-so-well-meaning colleague, who, after learning the topic of my dissertation, immediately pointed out: "You can't teach Proust to undergraduates." Since I was planning to make a career out of doing, at least in part, precisely that, I dismissed this comment at the time, but am dismayed now to find Proust-lovers from as diverse perspectives as Julia Kristeva and Harold Bloom suggesting that the modern reader has been MTV-ified into an impatient consumer of video clips and sound bites, incapable of understanding much less enjoying great literature. In her recent book on Proust, Kristeva suggests that film and television have left Proust "inaccessible" (1994, 290) to the modern reader, while Bloom blames "the proliferation of fresh technologies for distraction" for the "fact" that he now finds "only a few handfuls of students" who enter Yale with "an authentic passion for reading" (1994, 517, 519). If

Bloom cannot find reading-lovers at Yale, what are we to find in the provinces?

Alvin Kernan pushes this doomsaying to its logical conclusion in *The Death of Literature*, where he argues that the "literary enterprise" of which Proust is a prime example must give way under the corrosive influence of "a technological revolution that is rapidly transforming a print into an electronic culture" (1990, 9). All this would seem to suggest that core courses might wisely forgo advanced-level reading of works like Proust's in favor of more "assimilable" texts. Or better yet, films. Fortunately, however, the apparently common impression that the rise of television and film have tolled literature's death knell is not entirely supported by research into television's effect on reading.

In his review of the research, Stephen Krashen points out that moderate television-watching has only a slight effect on literacy (1993, 82). While it is true that excessive television-watching does not make for good readers, Krashen concludes that "it is not the presence of television that prevents children from reading; more likely, it is the absence of good books" (83). It would seem then that if we wish our students to develop the critical thinking skills necessary for good writing and analytical reading, we should present them with the challenge of reading the best literature available.

While it is true that Proust's three-thousand-page work is too long for most courses, I would suggest that *Combray,* the opening two hundred pages of *In Search of Lost Time,* presents just the sort of reading exercise we need to offer students–the joy and sheer pleasure of reading life's experiences beautifully reconstructed on a page. For students accustomed to the rapid-fire sensory bombardment of video clips, reading Proust bring together the disparate moments of his life may help them make sense of theirs.

I would not argue that we should include Proust in a course based solely on the thematic content on the novel, rich as it may be. This is not to belittle thematic considerations, but only to suggest that if we want to encourage students to read and reread, we must offer them readings whose poetry and linguistic passion excite their imagination. Although we cannot ignore the political, moral, and financial interests that converge in defining great literary works, our classes will most likely inspire more students to read on their own, if we emphasize literature's aesthetic distinctiveness, its use of language in what Robert Alter has described as "densely layered communication" (1989, 28). Few novels offer the complex reading experience of *In Search of Lost Time,* especially when read in its entirety over a period of weeks or months. When reading Proust, even in amounts more suitable to the classroom, one becomes keenly aware of the time spent reading and the experience of time as presented in the book. As readers, we remember our reading of the book as we read of Proust's remembrance. This effect is of course lessened in a reading of only part of the novel, yet it occurs throughout, and to no less an extent in *Combray.*

Toward the end of this first volume, after having presented the hero Marcel's childhood memories of the many hours he spent walking the Méséglise and Guermantes ways, Proust begins to build to a climatic crescendo designed at once to conclude and foreshadow. As the narrator reflects on the meaning of the events and memories he has described, he explains that certain impressions seem to take on a "charm, a significance which is for me alone" (Proust 1989, 202). He continues: "When, on a summer evening, the melodious sky growls like a tawny lion, and everyone is complaining of the storm, it is the memory of the Méséglise way that makes me stand alone in ecstasy, inhaling, through the noise of the falling rain, the lingering scent of invisible lilacs" (ibid.). Although some of the rhythmic balance of this sentence must be attributed to the translator's punctuation, which doubles the number of commas in the original French, the longing nostalgia for the "lingering scent of invisible lilacs" is nonetheless the sort of Proustian *tour de force* that we can rightly expect to capture our students' imagination. Read in context as literally a moment of stylistic and thematic climax, this sentence epitomizes the distillation of great writing that inspires readers to read on.

Thus to those who would argue that the modern reader is an oxymoron or that literature is dead, I would argue that we have only to provide the opportunity for students to discover their natural curiosity for language in reading. Although we may lament what we perceive as a decline in student interest in reading, I have found that students generally respect and respond to a good challenge, especially when presented with enthusiasm and conviction.

The notion, then, that Proust is "beyond" our students is defeatist in that it ignores the fact that reading is a learned skill, which like any other can only be acquired through practice. To the question, What are we to practice? I suggest Proust or any author whose writing stimulates the critical thinking and creativity we seek to teach. If students increasingly are coming into America's colleges and universities lacking in advanced-level reading skills, then we should challenge them with the sort of reading experiences that will develop creative minds capable of concentrating long enough to perform thoughtful analysis. Great writers demand creative readers. Proust asks his readers to read in themselves to make with him the cognitive and emotional connections he sees in life. Given what appears to be widespread pessimism concerning our students' ability to read the most challenging works, it is perhaps wise, when considering the relationship of "tradition and innovation" in the core curriculum, to remember that if students are to become alive to the demands of the new century, we might do well to read with them the best works of the old.

Works Cited

Alter, Robert. 1989. *The Pleasures of Reading in an Ideological Age.* New York: Simon and Schuster.

Bloom, Harold. 1994. *The Western Canon: The Books and School of the Ages.* New York: Harcourt Brace.

Kernan, Alvin. 1990. *The Death of Literature.* New Haven: Yale University Press.

Krashen, Stephen. 1993. *The Power of Reading: Insights from the Research.* Englewood, Colorado: Libraries Unlimited.

Kristeva, Julia. 1994. *Le Temps sensible: Proust et l'expérience littéraire.* Paris: Gallimard.

Proust, Marcel. 1989. *Swann's Way.* Translated by C.K. Scott Moncrieff and Terence Kilmartin. New York: Vintage.

Selection

Reading Together:

One Culture out of Many

Theodora Carlile

Saint Mary's College

A college, in both the root sense of the word and in its best sense, is a community. We come together to learn and to teach, not only because some are learned and some seek to become learned, nor simply because it is more efficient to teach to groups–or even because it is more enjoyable to learn together–but because a mutual exchange of ideas, a conversation, or an ongoing discourse among the members of a community is the very essence of education. Being together on one campus, however, does not alone create a coherent community of learning. Perhaps a common understanding of education, shared values, a similarity of backgrounds might form the basis for such cohesion. But this degree of homogeneity is not to be found, and surely not to be harkened after, in today's world.

In lieu of this I believe we can turn to reading, the reading of shared texts, and discussion of them, to weave the fabric of an educational community. Reading books together and talking together about them, especially those we often call great works, brings a clarity of focus to the mutual exchange. Those engaged in reading together find in these works catalysts for perceptive insights and heightened sensitivity. Moreover, the texts can yield a sort of vocabulary which will enable a high level of discourse in the community, providing, as it were, a new language, more subtle, articulate, and varied than the ordinary speech most of our students, and we ourselves, are in the habit of using.

At Saint Mary's College in our Collegiate Seminar Program we ask all our students, as well as faculty across five schools and numerous departments, to engage over four semester-length courses in the shared reading of core texts. For example, we read and discuss the beginnings of Euclid's *Elements* in Greek Thought Seminars. We grapple with what he means in defining a point as "That which has no Part." We ask the question, "Why start with that definition?" Moreover we work through the Definitions, Common Notions, and Postulates, and the first few theorems, noting the difficulties and pleasures of Euclid's scrupulous, logical organization of space. The sharing of this experience can have numerous possible repercussions for both faculty and students. In math and science classes, for example, instructors can be assured that a reference to Euclid will not be lost on the group. In questioning an axiomatic system, or discussing the concept of space, that shared text will enable the classroom dialogue to move further and resonate more authentically. Faculty, as well, find commonality in the shared texts. No matter what their disciplinary background or area of expertise, they share common interests and a common set of questions which enable them to engage in a discourse beyond campus politics or the latest newspaper headlines.

It helps that not only are the texts we read of great worth and merit, but they themselves often represent, and thus model for us, a conversation with each other. In the Western tradition, from which most of our texts are currently drawn, intertextuality is rich. What I would like to extol here, however, is not a list of core books which adheres merely to the "Great Books" of the Western tradition, but rather one which is open and inclusive of other traditions as well. There are several credible objections to such inclusion. One I have certainly implied. If our aim is to foster a community of learning and to engender a high level of discourse, the mutual interchange of ideas from text to text, then it is of value to select core texts from a unified tradition, one which will itself serve to model and nurture such discourse. A second very credible reason to adhere exclusively to the Western tradition is that most of us who teach know and have been trained in that tradition. To attempt to introduce our students to *The Bhagavad-Gita* or the *Popol Vuh*, for instance, is to risk engaging in a fool's errand, or worse, to risk belittling those works by treating them cavalierly or even as mere token texts.

However, as many agree, there are a number of powerful reasons why we should include texts from a diversity of traditions on our core lists. It is manifest that many other traditions besides the Western have rich, profound, and beautiful works, well worth a lifetime of reading and study. However, that texts are great and worthy of study is not a sufficient reason for inclusion. Within any one tradition there are a plethora of great works, so that determining which to exclude, and on what basis, is in reality the task we face in designing core lists. Nonetheless, several considerations suggest that the inclusion of texts from diverse traditions is a compelling principle.

First, and most obviously, our society itself is becoming increasingly diverse. The students who are entering our universities, and increasingly the faculty as well, have roots in cultures all across the globe. Courtesy and practicality both suggest that a diversity of traditions in those most honored core reading lists will serve as an invitation for diverse groups to readily join the community of learners. Who we are is changing and our notions of roots must change with that identity.

There is another reason for a multicultural core list, however, which is of a different order. If we can only engage in learning in a spirit of commonality, it is equally the case that we can only truly learn in an environment of originality. The essence of dialogue is difference. Terms from the past, used and re-used within the discourse, become calcified and overburdened with history. By bringing into the conversation a set of texts from other traditions, we enliven and re-invigorate our discourse. Moreover, we avail ourselves of the particular advantages of our own times, the richness of a global perspective.

Recently at a workshop for Saint Mary's Seminar faculty we read and discussed, over a two-day period, a series of readings related to poetry and the fine arts. Among the works discussed were Plato's *Ion* and several poems each by the Tang Dynasty poet Li Po. What struck many of us in talking about these poems was their resonance with, yet uncanny "shaking up" of, the terms in which we had been discussing *The Ion*. In reading "Seeing a Friend Off," for example, we noted an intriguing use of natural landscape and spatial imagery. The poem goes:

> Green hills sloping from the northern wall,
> white water rounding the eastern city:
> once parted from this place
> the lone weed tumbles ten thousand miles.
> Drifting clouds–a traveler's thoughts;
> setting sun–an old friend's heart.
> Wave hands and let us take leave now,
> *hsiao-hsiao* our hesitant horses neighing.[1]

In our discussion of Plato we had been concerned with the notion of a poet's special *techne*. We had questioned whether this expertise of the poet was, as Socrates seemed to be saying, an art of imitation relying directly on knowledge of the object, or an art of making metaphor or myth. In Li Po's verse neither alternative seemed quite to apply. The poet does not so much depict an image of the landscape, or even principally elicit an emotion through imagery, but rather constructs a moment of human consciousness–the human mind caught in the act of noting and feeling both the landscape and the simultaneous departure of the friend. The moment has a wholeness and a fullness and yet a pinpoint singularity which is not so much captured in the images of the poem as it *is* the poem. Though Li Po's poetry is part of a rich and ancient literary and intellectual culture, it is removed from the debates and discussions surrounding Plato's poetics. This removal adds both an uneasiness and a vigor to our encounter with the text. It is this combination of uneasiness and vigor which is, I believe, a prerequisite for true education.

Reading Li Po's poem, for example, can stir up and re-engage our interest in poetics. It can change our way of reading Plato. And it can help us understand Euclid, suggesting to us that, like the poem, Euclid's definition of a point may be not so much a depiction of a physical reality, nor even the image of an abstract idea, but the re-creation in the mind's activity of a dynamic state of consciousness more than an object. For those trained in the Western tradition it can change our way of reading ourselves.

Note
1. Li Po, "Seeing a Friend Off," *The Columbia Book of Chinese Poetry*, trans. and ed. Burton Watson (New York: Columbia University Press, 1984).

A House Divided:

History and Literature in the Interdisciplinary Humanities Course

David W. Chapman

Samford University

The growing support for a core curriculum, as evidenced by the membership in the Association for Core Texts and Courses, indicates the pressing need to provide a common foundation for a student's academic experience. Many of these core courses–particularly in the humanities–include texts and units of study drawn from various disciplines. Since core courses need not be interdisciplinary and, in the minds of some, should not be, it is important to consider the causes of their proliferation.

The most obvious answer may be administrative expediency. In a time of shrinking academic resources, the interdisciplinary course allows administrators to draw on a larger faculty pool in staffing introductory core courses. Furthermore, such courses may help reduce general education requirements–a move often welcomed by both students and faculty.

But the impetus for interdisciplinary courses is not entirely–perhaps not even fundamentally–about budgets and faculty lines. Advocates for a "great books" course from Mortimer Adler to Allan Bloom have generally favored an eclectic mix of literary, historical, and philosophical texts. Indeed, the very categories of modern university life seem hardly applicable to some works of the classical period. As Terry Eagleton reminds us, the traditional definition of literature was much broader than that invoked by contemporary departments of English (1983, 1-2). Until the twentieth century, letters and essays, sermons and lectures, narrative history and autobiography, were all crowded together under the heading of literature.

Stanley Fish notes that the pressure for interdisciplinarity comes from both the left and the right. The left often characterize disciplines in Marxist terms as "institutional structures by means of which the various academic disciplines establish and extend their territorial claims" (1989, 15). The right, on the other hand, attack disciplinary structures for promoting "the decline of culture in a world where all coherence is gone and the center has not held" (ibid.).

Although interdisciplinary courses may combine various disciplines in the sciences or social sciences, the most commonly offered course focuses on "civilization" or "culture" and includes primary readings from the humanities. It has been generally assumed that professors in the humanistic disciplines could teach Homer and Thucydides, Shakespeare and Descartes. Indeed, Adler's original intention was to bring together groups of interested readers without any formal academic training in the fields represented by these authors.

However, curricula, like utopia, are often better on paper than in practice. In order to demonstrate the difficulties encumbered in interdisciplinary course design, I want to illustrate with the problems encountered at my own university when faculty from the humanities, primarily history and English, were asked to develop an interdisciplinary core course.

Although Samford is a traditional liberal arts college which left its general education requirements relatively untouched since World War II, the winds of change began to blow over the campus in the 1990s. A faculty committee was set up to review the general education program and make recommendations for reform. The result was an ambitious fifty-five-hour core curriculum dubbed "Cornerstone." The Cornerstone program required students to complete six courses in Cultural Legacies as well as courses in mathematics, foreign language, science, fitness, and personal wholeness.

Each of the Cultural Legacies courses focused on primary texts and artifacts from the period being studied. Each of the courses included a mix of history, political science, literature, philosophy, art, music, and drama–albeit in varying proportions. Faculty for these courses were drawn from various departments on campus, although English and history predominated. Summer workshops funded by FIPSE and NEH grants allowed faculty to spend an extended period in reading and discussing the primary works and in course preparation.

After a six-year run, the program was scuttled by an administrative decree that had more to do with budgetary considerations than philosophical decisions. In its place (and I omit a lot of political maneuvering here) grew up Son of Cornerstone–a twenty-two-hour core program that included two semesters of Cultural Perspectives. In an attempt to expedite the course design, a triumvirate, consisting of one faculty member from English, one from religion, and one from history, was appointed to write the course description and select the texts. After several weeks of negotiation, the English representative withdrew, citing irreconcilable differences. The design group was then reduced to joint consuls–one from history, and a newly appointed one from English. Another round of negotiations began, but each proposal forwarded by English was vetoed by the history department, and vice versa. These "memo wars" are instructive of not only the animosity generated by competing visions for this course, but of the more general problems of interdisciplinary collaboration. In a cry, reminiscent of the French revolution, the issues were "ideology, chronology, and identity."

The first shoal encountered by those navigating the proposals was, unsurprisingly, ideology. The history and political science department tended to support the canonical works of Western civilization: Plato, Machiavelli, Adam Smith, Karl Marx. The English department swiftly rejected these dead, white, European, males as representatives of an unenlightened tradition in Western letters. Witness this e-mail response from one English faculty member: "The English faculty has been completely ignored, except for a few token texts. The course, as it is, is a standard, non-innovative Western civ course with a global footnote at the very end of the second semester."

In fact, the history department was not as conservative as the English department pictured them. First, the historians felt that these writers were important starting points for a discussion of intellectual history, rather than ideologues that would seduce the minds of the students. Second, the historians were less likely to insist that the author's gender and class overshadowed the ideas expressed in the work. Plato, for instance, explicitly rejected the notion that women were unfit to serve as philosopher-kings, yet he was rejected out of hand as a member of the male hierarchy. Finally, the historians noted that the primary works should be presented in the context of subsequent criticism, in some cases undermining the original intention of the author. Clearly, no one was advocating teaching Machiavelli in order to promote deceit and treachery. On the contrary, many thought that teaching the works of a political opportunist might be the best way to expose the danger of such an approach to life.

The historians were even more confused by the English department's attack on chronology. To the uninitiated, the organization of the English department appears to be largely historical. Anthologies generally follow a chronological arrangement. Professors are hired with such specializations as eighteenth-century English literature or twentieth-century American poetry. And traditional criticism often included a good bit of historical research. Where did Hawthorne get his idea for a scarlet letter? What did Shakespeare know about the succession of Scottish kings? However, under the influence of the New Historicists, literary criticism has grown to be more fluid, cutting across historical dividing lines in order to expose competing visions of reality. The history proposal and the English proposal were clearly distinguished by the importance of chronology as an organizing principle. As a result, the English department fired this shot over the bow in response to the history proposal:

> The English Department is emphatic in its opposition to the event-driven structure of the proposed course. There is a feeling in English that the event-centered structure of the proposal skews this course toward history. Since this course on Civilization is about the history of ideas, the English Department feels that ideas should be primary in the course proposal, supported by sub-topics (either events or themes) devised by the individual instructor.

The history department representative–a Southern historian–replied to the English challenge with a counterattack:

> I have only argued that ideas taken outside of context tend to float in the student's personal space–everything becomes immediately presentist, and there is no connection made with the past and no awareness that cultural conditions–including but not limited to the West, patriarchies, other cultures, matriarchies, etc.–influence both the genesis and the articulation of ideas....I have worked to "structure" the course around a chronology because that is consistent with the New Historicism, because it provides a workable framework by which a variety of instructors from all disciplines can teach, and most importantly because it allows us to go back to the past and bring it to the present without floating.

Although both the challenger and the respondent seem to advocate the same New Historical stance, they are, as their proposals indicated, quite divided on the way it affects course structure. The historians find the chronological structure to be the basis for a coherent course design. The English faculty, on the other hand, are committed to subverting chronological arrangements because they reinforce traditional notions about the past (e.g., the triumph of Western civilization).

Although the concerns over ideology and chronology were certainly "hot buttons" during the development of the Cultural Perspectives course, another issue lay at the root of much of the problem. Ultimately, most faculty felt disenfranchised with the course because they weren't allowed to pursue their own disciplines. The most consistent criticism of the course among history faculty is that it doesn't actually contain enough history, that too much of the course content is not anchored in a historical context, that it is "floating." Similarly, the most enduring and universal of the criticisms flowing from the English department is that the study of literature has been lost in the core curriculum. The department collectively mourns the loss of the required sophomore-level literature survey courses. They have, they feel, sold their birthright for a mess of pottage in the new curriculum.

What lessons can be learned from this morality play? First of all, those who suggest there is a natural affinity between English and history speak from deep ignorance. Although the divide may appear much less than between, say English and psychology, or history and biology, the disciplinary loyalties and organizational identities are just as deep, and perhaps more intense for being filial. Our deepest rivals are always our siblings.

Second, any interdisciplinary course will require extensive, and sometimes excruciating, dialogue among the participants. When actually gathered together in a single room, our English faculty and history faculty have much in common and are willing to work cooperatively. When working in isolation, however, the faculty tend to fall into their own entrenched disciplinary values. Put simply, it is much easier to dismiss a colleague's ideas if that colleague is not sitting across the table from you.

Finally, when differences do emerge, someone must play the role of mediator. Our course design was ultimately salvaged by a dean who was committed to making it work. He negotiated a series of compromises that ultimately made the course palatable, if not delectable, to both sides.

The new Cultural Perspectives course will be taught for the first time this fall, so the jury is still out on the most important questions: Will students find that the course really does lay the foundation for their collegiate experience? Will faculty undermine the course because they feel conscripted into teaching a course that is not to their liking? Will they subvert the interdisciplinary intent of the course by focusing on their own areas of expertise? Will our Cultural Perspectives course be the herald of a New Jerusalem or is it the sound of Armageddon I hear in the distance?

Works Cited
Eagleton, Terry. 1983. *Literary Theory*. Minnesota: University of Minnesota P.
Fish, Stanley. 1989. "Being Interdisciplinary Is So Very Hard to Do," *Profession*: 15-22.

The Staying Power of a
Little-Known Novella:

Ann Petry's "In Darkness and Confusion"

Jacqueline Wilkie and David Faldet

Luther College

We are part of the Paideia I program, a two-semester core require-ment for all first-year students at Luther College. The course is com-mitted by its mission statement in the Luther catalog to teach "significant texts." Since the course is team-taught by all the members of both the history and English departments, a group of twenty or more, the meaning of "significant" is understood somewhat differently by various team members. Essentially, for the history department "significant texts" open up a historical moment. These texts are primary sources used to draw students into a deeper understanding of the past and its relationship to the present. For the English department, "significant texts" aesthetically model important moral dimensions of the human experience. Jackie jokingly refers to the difference between history and English as the materialists versus the universalists.

Texts selected for inclusion in the course must in some way encom-pass the aims of both departments. One text that has done this with considerable success is Ann Petry's "In Darkness and Confusion," a novella that is not widely recognized as a classic in African-American literature, but has become a classic within our program. In this session on "Better than Other Narratives," we would like to argue that Petry's novella has proven better than other, better-known works of African-American fiction because it aesthetically engages and models a deeply moral dimension of human experience while engaging students in a deeper understanding of a clearly defined historical moment, and because it allows white, midwestern, middle-class students at Luther College to see African-Americans as like themselves, rather than as exotic "others." While not a classic in a canonical sense, Petry's "In Darkness and Confusion" is a Paideia I classic because it innovatively allows us to blend historical and literary study in one small body.

To understand our choice and use of the text you will need some background on the Paideia I course. Paideia I fulfills the one English and the one history requirement for all Luther students. Only a few transfer students are exempted from the course. And almost all are required to take the course in their first year (the only exceptions are some international students who first need to improve their language skills). Because first-year students all live in the same dorms, and because Luther is a residential college, Paideia becomes the academic center of a fairly intense year of community life. Unlike traditional womb-to-tomb Western civilization courses or great texts surveys, Paideia is divided by semesters into distinct, topical units. The first semester focuses on classical Athens and sixteenth-century Europe as two key moments in the development of the Western tradition. The second semester, a study of diversity in modern culture, begins with a unit on China since 1850 and concludes with a unit on American diversity developed mainly through study of Norwegian-Americans and African-Americans. This ordering of the units is a recent innovation. Ending with the American Diversity unit, about which students assume they know the most, has served well the goals of both the history and English departments.

The African-American section of which Petry's text is a part takes students on a journey both in time and the human experience. We begin our pilgrimage in captivity in Africa and experience the Middle Passage as told through the narrative of Olaudah Equiano. We survive slavery with Frederick Douglass and Harriet Jacobs, and grapple with the paradoxes of freedom and Reconstruction through the essays of Booker T. Washington and W. E. B. DuBois. Petry's novella and the works of Harlem Renaissance poets root us in the Northern, urban migration. The contrast between the hopes of African-Americans and their experiences in the 1940s sets the stage for the Civil Rights movement where we read Martin Luther King's "Letter from Birmingham Jail" and Malcolm X's speech "Message to the Grass Roots." The sub-unit and the course ends with a selection from a contemporary African-American writer which raises the question "Where do we go from here?"

In the twenty years the Paideia course has been in existence only the Frederick Douglass and Martin Luther King readings have remained continually on our syllabus. The next oldest selection is Petry. Petry's story is set in Harlem, on two hot summer days during the middle of World War II. It is about the family of William and Pink Jones, their niece Annie May, and their son Sam. The Joneses are good people. William and Pink both put in long hours at their jobs and do them well. But Pink remains at the beck and call of the family for which she serves as a domestic servant, and William is still called "boy" and limited to cleaning and shelving at the drugstore where he works.

They can't seem to afford a more spacious or accessible apartment, or a home less adjacent to the red-light district. Their niece Annie May has dropped out of school with a happy "good-bye" from the administration, and their son Sam has been drafted into service and sent to a boot camp in the deep South–a development that gives his Southern-born parents huge cause for anxiety.

In the middle of a summer heat wave Sam finds out that his son has been court-martialed for shooting an MP who tried to force him to the back of a Southern bus, and when Sam sees a Harlem policeman fire on a black serviceman who tries to defend a prostitute, his reactions help spark a riot among frustrated Harlem blacks. Pink, who is on her way back from church, also snaps in grief and anger when she hears about her son. Though a faithful choir member and teetotaler, she leads the rioters in breaking open a liquor store.

"In Darkness and Confusion" helps the largely white and often rural midwestern population of Luther students see, from a personal angle, an important moment in African-American history. We use the story to introduce the Northern migration of African-Americans which began in the nineteen-teens. We explore the results of this migration in the cultural blossoming of the Harlem Renaissance and the integration of Africa-American experience into the national (as opposed to the Southern) character.

The novella also provides us with an opportunity to talk about "race matters" in the U.S. in the twentieth century. For example, the U.S. historians on our teaching staff are concerned that students understand the meaning of race riots in the history of the nation. Many of our students assume that such riots are all like the "Rodney King Riots," the racial conflict with which they are most familiar. Some on our staff survey the riots of the 1920s, 40s, and 60s to illustrate that whites have been as likely to start rioting as blacks, and that different riots are about more than black economic deprivation upon which white, liberal journalists dwell in the media. The stories of Annie May, Pink, and Sam put a human face on the rioter and reinforce the message that not all riots are the same, and not all rioters are motivated by economic desires or frustrations.

The novella also meets another pedagogic aim of members of both departments: it provides access to women's lives through the words of a woman author. Throughout the year we try to see women's experiences and hear women's voices within each unit, something of a challenge in the first semester. Petry's novella is the first lengthy piece of serious fiction by a woman that many of our students have read. The staying power of the novella may in some way be attributed to the human depth of Petry's female characters, who challenge racial and sexual stereotypes directly. If Pink is a mammy, she is a "mammy with an attitude," and her pride is as much connected to her Christian righteousness as it is to the meticulousness of her dress. If Annie May is a loose woman, she also has a cynical wit, a day job, and dreams of something better. And the brave among the staff may even attempt to use Petry to talk about the concept of the male gaze, since we are introduced to two Pinks and two Annie Mays–the ones we see through Sam's eyes and the ones we see through each woman's own actions.

The Paideia course went through several years of reading an additional better-known work of fiction by a woman author. Zora Neale Hurston's *Their Eyes Were Watching God* deals with the same period of history. It raised complaints among staff, however, because it is set in an exceptional black community in rural Florida and reinforces some negative white stereotypes of African-Americans, in particular of African-American women. While Hurston was popular with some students, for many the dialect and mythic structure of the story was too foreign to draw them fully into the historical moment of the early twentieth-century South.

The length of Petry's novella, and the fact that it is part of an African-American anthology that's been in print for close to thirty years, has also figured into our choice. Yet Richard Wright's novella, "The Man Who Lived Underground," is in the same anthology, and is reprinted from the *Cross-Section* anthology of 1944, where Petry's came out three years later, in 1947. While Wright's novella engages philosophically with the social and psychological forces of oppression that also figure in Petry's novella, his work is staged on a more mythic level–pushing history to the background in depicting the black urban hell of twentieth-century America. Petry and her novella are less well-known than Wright, whose novella connects back to the philosophical tradition of Dostoevsky and looks forward to the classic African-American everyman story, Ralph Ellison's *Invisible Man*, but the existentialist point of Wright's novella makes a sharp contrast to the down-to-earth family problems of Petry's text.

Part of the challenge of teaching a historical moment is pulling students out of their familiar frame of present reference. "In Darkness and Confusion" begins by touching on some familiar points of reference for our students, but it quickly pulls them into the unfamiliar ground of paradox. Our students know about World War II, the war into which Sam Jones has been called to serve, but they know it as a righteous war against fascism and the powers of hate in Europe and against imperialism in the Pacific. What they don't recognize is the racism at work within the U.S. armed forces in which Sam Jones serves, a racism that segregates and oppresses. This paradox of history, a racist fighting force fighting Hitler's racism, draws our students into a deeper sense of the perspective of 1940s Harlem. So too our students know and participate in their own family narratives of the American dream of upward mobility. In Petry's story our mostly white, midwestern students may begin with an outsider's distance on the smell of straightening irons and the spectacle of an overweight black woman who has trouble getting out of bed. Once they see that William and Pink Jones are hardworking and decent people, however, they find themselves facing an ethical paradox: should such people remain silent while not only they but also their children are thwarted and hurt by an economic and political system with glaring double standards? The familiarity of the Joneses' values helps students begin to see African-Americans as "us," not "them": even students who can honestly say they have never lived in the same town with or spoken to an African-American before coming to Luther.

The American Diversity unit as a whole and the Petry reading in particular have fared well in student evaluations of the course. In a course where students brag, "I learned to skim texts and b.s. my way through papers," most students report that they not only read but enjoyed Petry. In last year's evaluation by randomly selected first-year students, one person asserted, "Readings for this unit truly captured my attention and interest. I never read this much in Paideia before." Another simply stated, "Petry excellent." Additionally, students seem to understand the purpose of the Diversity unit in ways they do not understand the other parts of the course. One student summarized, "This material is vital for all of us to be aware of and understand our American community better." Part of the student identification with the materials in this section of the course is that it brings closer a moment in history that students feel to be connected with their own lives. The literature we have chosen makes that moment incarnate.

When literature professors seek to stick to the classics of tradition there is a danger of favoring works that have distanced themselves from history. In our own course, it is always tempting to stress the travels and other worldly tests of Odysseus over the more time-bound testing of rules of hospitality as Odysseus confronts the suitors, or to stress the imaginative construction of Utopia in Book Two of More's work, over the conversation in Belgium that precedes it in Book One. Conversely, it is tempting for historians to focus exclusively on the moment in time and the material conditions which produced the sources we are reading. We are tempted to explore the details of Herodotus' sources and his construction of a historical narrative and yet ignore the moral questions he raises about human nature. The makeup of the teaching faculty in Paideia forces us to resist both these temptations. Literary specialists must face the material conditions and historians must cope with aesthetics and moral dilemmas, and the texts we use must allow us to do both at once. This dynamic tension has created a course based on texts that move students beyond disciplinary knowledge to deeper integrated understanding of what it means to be human at different points in different places in time.

Accessible Science:

Mendel in a Sequence of Core Science Papers

Thomas A. Huber

Mercer University

The origins of plant breeding probably predate the origins of organized agriculture (Corcos and Monaghan, 38). Analysis of plant remains from both the Old and the New World indicates that currently used domesticated plants were already far different from their wild ancestors as far back as three thousand to six thousand years ago. Thus, there are few human activities that shape deliberately the species with which we most intimately live that are more traditional than plant breeding. And yet, for thousands of years, plant breeding was more an art, and not yet a science. Breeding took place without the application of the knowledge of cells or plant sexuality or chromosomes or genes. These concepts would not enter scientific discussions until the eighteenth, nineteenth, and twentieth centuries.

As John Moore (252) has pointed out, two main lines of research lead to the study of inheritance: plant hybridization and cytology, especially as the latter eventually came to focus on the "behavior" of chromosomes. The first of these lines of research predates history, although it may have contributed to, or at least benefited from, the invention of record-keeping and, thus, writing. The latter of these can be more precisely dated to 15 April 1663, when Robert Hooke demonstrated to the Royal Society the "invisible" cellular structure of cork. Only in the years 1902 to 1903 would the implications of these two lines of research first be combined in a brilliant pair of papers by Walter Sutton, and in 1931 would the final synthesis become incarnate in that "cornerstone" of experimental genetics, "A correlation of cytological and genetical crossing-over in *Zea mays*" by Harriet Creighton and Barbara McClintock (Peters, 27; 155).

But, as every one here knows, we can see clearly the direction of the arrow that points toward the modern knowledge of genetics when we read carefully the seminal paper in that field, Gregor Mendel's "Experiments in Plant Hybridization." Mendel's work represents the culmination of a concern with plant hybridization, and the beginning of an approach that was commensurate with the approaches emerging in the field of cytology.

I need to take a moment to explain my history with these topics and how Mendel's monumental paper can play a role in a core text curriculum. Mercer University, where I teach, has a Great Books program as one of two general education tracks. This program was modeled in form after the curriculum at St. John's in Annapolis and Sante Fe, although at Mercer it is a nine course sequence that represents, perhaps, twenty-five percent of a student's academic work. Dr. John Stege of the English department and I were asked to design the last course in this sequence, a course that focuses on the early twentieth century. As far as scientific texts for the course were concerned, we were pulled between what one calls the "physics story" and the "genetics story." We knew, however, that students would have read selections from Darwin's *Origin of Species* in the previous course, and we felt that a level of mathematics unobtained by most of our Great Books students was necessary for really appreciating Einstein, Heisenberg, and others. Accordingly, we designed a sequence of eleven papers in genetics, starting with the previously mentioned paper by Mendel and ending with the short, but startling, paper by Watson and Crick from 1953 proposing a molecular structure for DNA. These papers are all found in the wonderful collection edited in 1959 by James A. Peters titled *Classical Papers in Genetics*, now, sadly, out of print and mostly unavailable.

Given that Mendel's paper can be dated to 1900 for its rediscovery and influence on the field of genetics, these papers chronicle the accelerating increase in our knowledge of inheritance. They also provide reasonably accessible reading for undergraduate students in the primary literature of a field of biology that makes headline after headline to this day in the popular press. Finally, the analytical thinking necessary for scientific endeavors, the ingenuity required to design and carry out experiments that address critical and imaginative questions posed by the researcher, and the complexity of the tapestry woven to position each additional thread of observation, are more apparent in this sequence of papers than any other of which I am aware–but back to Mendel.

A careful reading and discussion of Mendel's paper can illuminate several features of scientific inquiry. I wish to mention seven of these, and very briefly say a few words about each. First: There are fundamental assumptions underlying the activity of science that have been articulated by many scientists and philosophers of science. Some of these assumptions are clearly represented or articulated in Mendel's paper–expecting discernible regularity (or orderliness) in nature; searching for constant relationships (or laws) of a qualitative and quantitative nature; and supposing that what is true with one species may be true with others–and suggest that Mendel worked within these fundamental assumptions of science. For example, Mendel writes that "one might assume, however, that no basic difference could exist in important matters since unity in the plan of development of organic life is beyond doubt" (Corcos and Monaghan, 161).

Second: The importance of using an appropriate experimental organism for the question being asked is apparent in Mendel. Mendel writes that the

> experimental plants must necessarily: 1. Possess constant differing traits. 2. Their hybrids must be protected from the influence of all foreign pollen during the flower period or easily lend themselves to such protection. 3. There should be no marked disturbances in the fertility of the hybrids and their offsprings in successive generations. (Corcos and Monaghan, 63)

In addition, it also is apparent that the plants must be grown easily and with a minimum of space; they must reproduce rapidly; and they must reproduce in large numbers.

Third: The importance of technical terms, abstract symbolic notation, and descriptive statistics is obvious, but not overwhelming, in Mendel's paper. This is especially obvious after having previously read Darwin on inheritance, where technical terms, abstract symbolic notation, and descriptive statistics are, for the most part, absent. Phrases like dominating character, recessive character, parental character, and hybrid character take on new and important specific meanings. Only by distinguishing by name two characters that *appear* identical (dom-inating parental character and hybrid character) can one next question whether they might have differing causes. And this subtlety in Mendel's mind is perhaps the clearest mark of his brilliance. Also, Mendel's method of symbolically representing crosses simplified the information and made it easier to think about it. Finally, Mendel's knowledge of the importance of the mean (average) as the best representative value of a large number of observations, and the relationship between sample size and accuracy and precision, make it clear that he attempts to apply statistical methodology to his experimentation.

Fourth: The unexpected ability of a theory to explain other, seemingly unrelated observations, thus increasing the "power," validity, and believability of the theory, is seen in Mendel's paper. Mendel was able to explain the tendency of hybrids to revert to their parental types when reproduced by self-fertilization for several generations by using his developmental series law over several generations.

Fifth: The ability of the results of one study to direct or impact research in newer studies becomes clear when the other papers are read after Mendel's. In his conclusion, Mendel talks about the "elements" that are combined during fertilization from each of the gametes; however, he was not able to describe the *nature* of these elements. It is apparent that he believed them to be material and constant. Only later would chromosomes, and then genes, be determined as the physical forms of the carriers of the information. This sequence of discoveries becomes apparent when the entire set of papers is carefully read.

Sixth: Mendel was a reductionist, in that, unlike previous experimenters including Darwin, he only looked at one or two or three characters at a time, rather than at the collection of characters. This required that Mendel think that characters of organisms are in some way *independent* of the whole organism in a manner not previously recognized. Instead of seeing an offspring related to both parents in some portion of the appearance of its characters, Mendel saw *individual* characters like only *one* of the parents. In this way, he quickly moved past any notion of blending of characters in the offspring, just as the results of reciprocal crosses eliminated the possibility of preformation of the offspring. Several hundred years of preconceptions about plant breeding were overcome in the fertile garden of this great mind.

And seventh: The distinction between empirical laws and theoretical laws (or hypotheses) can clearly be made with Mendel, and then followed through with the subsequent papers. This distinction can be developed by bringing out the distinction between his various empirical laws describing the formation and development of hybrids over several generations and his theoretical law that sought to explain how germs cells *might* be constituted in order to give rise to the observed empirical laws. The assumptions leading up to his theoretical law describe the probable means and sequence of events for producing egg cells and sperm cells in pea plants. I won't state these laws, except to say that the theoretical laws describe a mechanism by which "hybrids produce germinal and pollen cells that correspond in equal numbers to all the constant forms resulting from the combination of traits united through fertilization" (Corcos and Monaghan, 141). With the addition of biographical material, one can also beautifully address the issue *why*

Mendel was able to revolutionize the study of inheritance. As Orel (1984) and Stern and Sherwood (1966) make clear, Mendel was trained as a physicist and mathematician. And in the years he studied his peas and applied what he had learned in these other fields of study, Mendel was an interdisciplinarian of the highest order.

Works cited

Corcos, Alain F. and Floyd V. Monaghan. 1993. *Gregor Mendel's Experiments on Plant Hybrids: A Guided Study.* New Brunswick, New Jersey: Rutgers University Press.

Moore, John A. 1993. "Mendel and the Birth of Genetics." *Science as a Way of Knowing: The Foundations of Modern Biology.* Cambridge, Massachusetts: Harvard University Press.

Orel, Vitezslav. 1984. *.Mendel.* Oxford: Oxford University Press.

Peters, James A., ed. 1959. *Classic Papers in Genetics.* Englewood Cliffs, New Jersey: Prentice-Hall.

Stern, Curt and Eva R. Sherwood, eds. 1966. *The Origin of Genetics: A Mendel Source Book.* San Francisco: W. H. Freeman and Company.

Uses of Technology with Core Texts:

The Case of "Virtual" v. "Wet" Labs

Ellen Belton

Brooklyn College of the City University of New York

The revolutions in electronic and multimedia technology are already transforming the way teachers teach and students learn. In light of the theme of this year's ACTC conference, it seems not only appropriate but important to examine the relationship between the traditional curriculum content of core programs and the innovative and rapidly evolving pedagogies resulting from the development of new educational technologies. My particular focus will be on the potential benefits and pitfalls associated with the uses of multimedia, Web sites, and other technologies to create distance-learning modules or even entire courses in a core program. On the assumption that the discussion currently taking place at my own institution can serve as an interesting example for others, and in the hope that the specifics I am going to relate will generate a broader discussion among the members of ACTC, I will first look at the process that has been unfolding over the last few years and then describe the debate in which we have recently been engaged over the role of technology in the laboratory component of core courses in the physical sciences.

For the past two years at Brooklyn College a self-selected group of faculty drawn from ten of the eighteen to twenty academic departments whose faculty regularly participate in the teaching of our ten-course

Core Curriculum have been working cooperatively on a range of projects designed to integrate distance-learning technologies into their teaching. These projects, known collectively as "WebCore," have used a variety of media ranging from e-mail groups to interactive tutorial programs and Web pages. With one exception, however, these projects have focused on the uses of technology as enhancements rather than replacements for real-time, face-to-face classroom instruction.

Then in Fall 1996, the President of Brooklyn College challenged the faculty to undertake the creation of a Virtual Core, a "high quality General Education curriculum that is free of time and space." I was asked to chair a task force that would take a leadership role in this work. The charge to the task force calls, initially, for the development of experimental components or of entire courses in at least four different core disciplines that could be offered on-line using new technologies such as e-mail, multimedia and the Web. The long-term goal is the development of distance-learning versions of as many courses in our Core Curriculum as can be offered in that format without in any way compromising academic quality.

Of course, as one of my colleagues on the task force recently put it, in spite of the fact that many faculty members view the notion of distance learning with anxiety or alarm, one powerful tool of distance learning—namely, the book—has been with us for much longer than most of us realize. Nonetheless, recognizing that we are still in the early stages of what promises to be a technological revolution of equal magnitude with the invention of the printing press, the task force has approached its work with a mixture of enthusiasm and trepidation. Charged with identifying and making recommendations on important policy matters, the task force has been considering issues such as faculty workload and incentives, intellectual property and course ownership, virtual class size, student credits, the impact of college, university, and state regulations and requirements, evaluation of various technologies, questions of the degree of distance within the Virtual Core structure, and methods of evaluation of new and experimental sections of Virtual Core courses. We recognize as well that as a commuter institution, the majority of whose students have family incomes of less than twenty thousand dollars a year, it is imperative that the college provide on-campus access and technical support for students who enroll in distance-learning versions of core courses.

I will now zero in on one issue that has been the occasion of considerable debate among the faculty and staff most actively engaged in developing the pilot Virtual Core projects. From the outset of the task force's work, it has been apparent that one of the initial pilot projects would be in the core biology course, since one of the faculty members who teaches that course, Prof. John Blamire, had already begun incorporating multimedia technology into his classroom presentations and had been providing supplementary materials for students in his laboratory sections on a biology core Web page. Last semester Professor Blamire replaced one of the lab modules with an interactive distance-learning program that he designed, and he was in the process of developing three or four additional interactive units. This semester Professor Blamire and two of his colleagues are teaching experimental sections of the biology core course in which three of the seven required lab sessions are being taught as interactive distance-learning modules.

The implementation of this pilot project has occasioned a lively discussion among members of the task force and within some of the core science departments. One member of the task force posed his concerns in the form of the following policy recommendation: "Courses which include credit for a laboratory component may satisfy that component with computer-simulated virtual laboratories up to, but not exceeding, one half of the total hours or laboratory meetings in the course." The rationale offered in support of this proposal acknowledges the practical advantages of virtual laboratories in terms of conservation of resources, exposure of students to new technology and opportunities for "the inclusion of experimental protocols which may be too time consuming, expensive, manually difficult or even dangerous for students to carry out by conventional means." These advantages, however, must be weighed against the educational benefits of students' handling actual laboratory materials and appreciating the difficulties of laboratory work and the nature of experimental error.

The discussion of this proposal among members of the task force, which has taken place almost entirely through e-mail, has been wide-ranging and constructive. Some faculty members in the humanities and social sciences have seen the concept of limiting the percentage of virtual material in core lab sections as applying to the concept of a Virtual Core in general. In fact, most of the faculty I have talked with, including most members of the task force, find it very difficult to imagine that their own core course could ever become totally virtual.

The discussion has also prompted several task force members who did not major in one of the natural sciences to reflect back with a mixture of fondness and chagrin on their own misadventures in the lab sessions of their required undergraduate science courses. One task force member, recalling her mishaps with a dissection module, asks:

> Would I have been better off dissecting a virtual dogfish? Probably not. Would I have preferred it? Probably so. In any case, the experience would have been very different–more controlled, less subject, for good or ill, to accidents, anomalies and simple incompetence. On the other hand, a

different type of lab experience might have adapted very well to virtual technology.

Another member, whose field is computer science, acknowledges the uniqueness of the hands-on physical lab experience but adds that "the world is changing, including experimental apparatus. Is the physical aspect of the lab experience truly as academically central as it used to be? Is it not being displaced, at least in some fields, by other areas and/or skills of importance?"

Although members of the task force continue to disagree about whether to limit the number of hours of computer-simulated virtual laboratories in science courses with a laboratory component, we have reached a consensus that at this stage in the development of a Virtual Core program it would be a mistake to put prior constraints on the experimental courses faculty members are designing. As one member of the task force puts it, it is important for the college to realize that

> we are not simply "putting courses on the Web." We're trying to deconstruct and rebuild courses. In doing so, [we] should [not] feel pressure to achieve x, y, or z percent of "virtuality." The classroom component isn't going to disappear soon. If and when it does, it will be because students are learning more, in different ways, and perhaps enjoying it more, too, along with their instructors. Each course should, and will, develop differently. Our goal is to teach the best Core possible with every means at our disposal, not to satisfy a percentage requirement of virtuality, whether it be 10% or 100%.